"This rich and carefully structured study of Luther's 'masks of God' offers precisely the kind of confessional Lutheran theology our churches need in an age of confusion about where and how God is at work in the world. Grounded in the distinction between the hidden and revealed God and in the centrality of Christ's incarnation as the only saving self-disclosure of the Father, the author traces how God binds himself to his chosen instruments: the external word, the sacraments, and his concrete 'signs' in history. By attending closely to Luther's exegesis of Genesis and his teaching on the ministry of the word, law and Gospel, the true and the false church, and God's ordering of home, church, and civil government, this work unfolds a profoundly evangelical vision that is thoroughly in harmony with the Scriptures and the Lutheran Confessions."

—Douglas L. Rutt
Professor Emeritus, Concordia Seminary, St. Louis

"According to Luther, the God who 'made me and all creatures' works in creation through the instrumentality of other creatures. That is, he 'hides' himself behind coverings or masks to accomplish his purposes in both the temporal and spiritual realms. Dr. Anthony Steinbronn has provided readers with a robust study of this key aspect of Luther's theology through a careful examination of his Genesis lectures and other texts. *The Masks of God* is an especially welcome addition to the growing body of research on Luther's doctrine of vocation. It will be of benefit to pastors and teachers who desire to deepen their understanding of Reformation theology for preaching and catechesis. The book's lucid style also makes it accessible to the general reader as well."

—John Pless
Assistant Professor of Pastoral Ministry and Missions, Concordia Theological Seminary, Ft. Wayne

"With the wisdom and skill of a seasoned teacher and pastor, Steinbronn offers us an insightful, comprehensive, and winsome account of Luther's theology of revelation. Using the Reformer's insight that God makes himself known in and through his masks in the world, Steinbronn outlines the various ways in which God reveals and enacts his purposes for creation in Christ through external signs of his will and word in the church and the world. Highly recommended as an entrée into the relevance of Luther's great insight for all of life."

—Leopoldo Sanchez
Professor of Systematic Theology, Concordia Seminary, St. Louis

"Books on Martin Luther's theology are usually intended for an academic audience and are inaccessible to those outside the guild. This one is not. Coherently, digestibly, and with a pastoral and evangelical tone, Anthony Steinbronn traces the thought of Luther on important topics that touch the whole of Christian life—Scripture, law and gospel, sacraments, church, family, government. You do not need previous knowledge of Luther, or even theology, to read this book and appreciate Luther's concern for the word of God permeating all of creation through the 'masks' that God has appointed for that purpose."

—Richard J. Serina Jr
Associate Executive Director, Commission on Theology and Church Relations, Lutheran Church Missouri Synod

The Masks of God

The Masks of God

Martin Luther's Use of Larvae Dei *in His Genesis Commentaries*

ANTHONY JAMES STEINBRONN

Foreword by Robert Kolb

WIPF & STOCK · Eugene, Oregon

The Masks of God
Martin Luther's Use of *Larvae Dei* in His Genesis Commentaries

Wipf & Stock
An Imprint of Wipf and Stock Publishers
199 W. 8th Ave., Suite 3
Eugene, OR 97401

www.wipfandstock.com

PAPERBACK ISBN: 979-8-3852-5569-6
HARDCOVER ISBN: 979-8-3852-5570-2
EBOOK ISBN: 979-8-3852-5571-9

VERSION NUMBER 031726

To the special "masks" through whom the Lord, in his goodness, has blessed my life:

to my parents, Reuben and Anna

to my wife and partner, Carol Susan

to my children, Leah Ruth, Joseph Reuben, Joshua Mark, and Jonathan David

God is the Poet, and we are the verses or songs He writes.

—MARTIN LUTHER (*LUTHER'S WORKS*, 7:366)

Contents

Foreword

WHO IS THAT MASKED God? In the midst of a turbulent world, with troubles and tribulations of assorted kinds assaulting us and tripping us up, we sense—we hope—that there must be someone or something pulling the strings, even when we feel at least a little bit confident that we can stand on our own two feet. But whatever or whoever it is eludes us. Our imaginations fashion workable concepts of an Ultimate or Absolute—or several—that help us hold life together—until they fall apart.

When the way he had been taught to think about how to secure life fell apart, Martin Luther came to realize that he needed to listen. He learned to stop actively trying to construct a ladder to heaven and instead to relay passively and listen to God's voice. Through the voice of his word his Creator let Brother Martin know who he really is. As controversy swirled around his Ninety-Five Theses on the practice of selling indulgences that offered forgiveness of sins, he formulated another series of theses to explain how he was practicing the interpretation of Holy Scripture. He took them to Heidelberg in April 1518 and shared with his Augustinian brothers his fresh insights into what God was telling him in Scripture.

Luther spoke of God Hidden—he did not use the term "mask" in these Heidelberg Theses—and God Revealed. In front of God Hidden he placed a "no entry," a "no trespassing" sign. God Hidden is God the Creator beyond the grasp and imagination of his human creatures. Trying to figure his dimensions can only result in, to use a concept from Ludwig Feuerbach, our fashioning a picture of the Ultimate and Absolute that reflects our own image.[1]

We know only what God has told us as he himself came into human flesh. And as Luther wrote, commenting on the Magnificat in 1521, "Since God is the Most High, and there is nothing above him, he cannot look above him; nor yet to either side, for there is none like him. He must, therefore, look within and beneath him; and the farther one is beneath him, the better does he see him."[2] It is only when we are being seen by God from his Creator's throne that we can see and hear him, Luther firmly believed.

Luther believed that God remains masked as he works in human history. Even when we have some sense that he is there and that he is acting, the course of human events often causes us to ask whether he is on our side, and perhaps more often to guess that he must be angry with us or indifferent to us or that he has gone on vacation. In some instances, in the face of life's tragedies and distresses and dilemmas, we will never find a plausible explanation for why and how he is dealing with us. God Hidden remains beyond our comprehension.

At the same time God has revealed himself. He has not only looked down upon us from the heights; he has come down among us, in the human language proclaimed and recorded by prophets, evangelists, and apostles, and in his own human flesh, in the mystery of his incarnation as Jesus of Nazareth. God Revealed, however, sometimes appears and talks to us in ways that seem strange. It is as if he hides himself in order to communicate with us most effectively, on our level.

For instance, the last place you would go looking for God is as a kid in a crib, or as a criminal on a cross, or as a corpse in a crypt. The strangest place to listen for all you need to know about and from God is in a little book of a few hundred pages, depending on the size of type, sometimes on paper of declining quality. The most curious way to encounter God is in simple water that is actually not just plain water only but water used as the setting for God to

1. Feuerbach, *Essence of Christianity.*

2. Luther, *Luther's Works*, 21:300.

express his promise of life everlasting. The oddest invitation we ever receive is to come to feast on the one who has prepared the meal, taking simple bread and ordinary wine that promise forgiveness of sins, life, and salvation because these elements of everyday life convey his body and blood. God reveals himself in ways unexpected, we might even say baffling—impossible to believe unless his Holy Spirit in a mysterious move clarifies for us how he operates as a multimedia communicator.

In this volume Anthony Steinbronn combines a lifetime interest in the teachings of Martin Luther with years of experience of acquainting people with Jesus of Nazareth, God in human flesh and blood, and facilitating their getting acquainted with the Creator who has liberated us from all the evils that infect us, all the burdens that threaten to crush us. Steinbronn did not cease to engage Holy Scripture and the writings of Martin Luther when his formal theological education came to an end. He actively pursued his interest in the Wittenberg way of thinking and preaching as he carried Christ's message to Africa and then to North America, as he echoed the proclamation of the prophets, evangelists, and apostles in his own preaching and ministering to God's people.

The author invites readers to join him in roaming through Luther's exposition of God's word and exploring with the reformer just how God has interacted with his human creatures, sharing their history as his own history, in a relationship in which he has remained faithful even when his people have not. Steinbronn perceives that God's mask cannot be stripped away in many of the experiences of daily life. He also lets readers know that we can rest assured, as Luther has said, that God Hidden is not a different person from God Revealed, as Jesus of Nazareth, as the crucified and resurrected second person of the Holy Trinity. As Luther reminds his students,

> "From an unrevealed God I will become a revealed God. Nevertheless, I will remain the same God. I will be made flesh, or send My Son. He shall die for your sins and shall rise again from the dead. And in this way I will fulfill your desire, in order that you may be able to know whether you are predestined or not. Behold, this is my

> Son; listen to him (cf. Matt. 17:5). Look at him as he lies in the manger and on the lap of his mother, as he hangs on the cross. Observe what he does and what he says. There you will surely take hold of me." For "he who sees me," says Christ, "also sees the Father himself" (cf. John 14:9). If you listen to him, are baptized in his name, and love his Word, then you are certainly predestined and are certain of your salvation.[3]

Whether we can easily perceive the God behind the mask or not, we need not second guess God Revealed, even with his masks, on the basis of our speculation about what God Hidden may be doing.

Questions about what kind of God it is who comes to us behind impenetrable masks in the march of history or behind see-through masks as Jesus the Messiah arise daily in life. The Holy Spirit is continually turning us back to Scripture and beckoning to us to let him accompany us into conversation with our Creator. Steinbronn's studies of the individual Christian life and our life together as his people, his body, in his church, will enliven our interest in and our dedication to listening to God as he reveals himself through his word that communicates life to us in its oral, written, and sacramental forms. The author engages us readers with questions that we face in daily life, and he aids us in joining Luther in plumbing the depths of the mysteries of God's revelation of himself.

Readers who proceed into the following pages will be blessed, challenged, informed, and inspired by the message and models of people like Noah, Abraham, Jacob, Joseph, John, Peter, and Paul, as well as by the person of the Lord Jesus himself. For Steinbronn lets Luther draw us into conversation with those whom the Holy Spirit has used and continues to use to bring life and salvation, healing and wholeness, death to sin and life in Christ to us. That is the adventure into which Steinbronn now leads us.

Robert Kolb
Wittenberg, Fifth Sunday after Pentecost 2025

3. Luther, *Luther's Works*, 5:45.

Preface

THE THEME FOR THIS book, the masks of God, was gleaned from a lecture by Dr. Eugene Klug back in 1989. That theme, two years later, became the focus of my master of sacred theology thesis, titled "The Masks of God: The Significance of *Larvae Dei* in Luther's Theology."

As a result of our sinful human nature, there can be no unmediated relationship between God and human beings, for God must wear a mask in all of his dealings with us. Therefore it is the responsibility of every person to apprehend him where, and in what manner, God has chosen to make himself known.

Foremost of these masks is his incarnation, the will of his good pleasure,[1] in which we are able to look into the very heart and will of the Father; and there we see that God is compassionate and does not desire the death of a sinner, but that the sinner should have eternal life (Luke 19:10; John 3:13–17).

In order that the peoples of the earth can be blessed, God clothes himself in the form of an ordinary person, like you and me, in order to accomplish his work on earth. Just as faith constitutes the proper relationship of a person to God, so good works and love define a person's relationship to one's neighbor of all kinds.

1. Luther, *Luther's Works*, 2:48.

Acknowledgment

Thank you to Robert Kolb . . . a "special mask" to the world of Reformation and Luther studies through whom we, for over a generation, have experienced the Lord's gracious face and blessing through Bob's erudite scholarship and evangelical churchmanship.

Introduction

Central Theme and Chapter Summaries

Central Theme

As a result of our sinful nature, there can be no unmediated relationship between God and human beings, for God must wear a mask in all of his dealings with us. Therefore it is the responsibility of every person to apprehend him where, and in what manner, he has chosen to make himself known.

Chapter 1: The Masks of God

"Man shall not see me and live" (Exod 33:20). As a result of our sinful nature human beings cannot see God, in his naked transcendence, and survive. Therefore since the fall of humankind into sin, there can be no unmediated relationship between God and human beings. God must wear a mask in all of his dealings with us.

Moreover, this nature of ours has become so misshapen through sin that it cannot recognize God, nor comprehend his nature, without a covering. Therefore God, in his grace and mercy, envelops himself in his word and works and seeks to reveal himself to us in certain forms. These concrete forms of the Holy Spirit are God's way to us and are a rejection of every way from man to God; for they are the common epiphanies for all people.

Thus the Holy Spirit's ministry is thoroughly external and completely available to our senses. God could have saved the human race in another way but it was his will to save us, and to reveal himself, in this way. Since the Holy Spirit works nothing without externals, it is the responsibility of every human being to apprehend him where, and in what manner, he has chosen to make himself known.

Luther offers several reasons why God comes to us through his concrete Spirit: (1) since the beginning of the world, divine wisdom has so ordained and arranged things that there is always some public sign toward which all people might look in order that they might find, worship and pray to the true God and be saved; (2) these outward and visible signs have been placed alongside the word so that human beings, reminded by the sign, would believe with greater assurance that God is kind and merciful and that he is with us, takes care of us, and is favorably inclined toward us; (3) since we cannot ascend to him, he has chosen to come to us and reveal himself within the range of our comprehension so that he can be found and known; (4) as God comes to us in these concrete forms, he deals with us in a twofold manner, first outwardly, through the oral word of the gospel and through material signs; then inwardly, through the work of the Holy Spirit, faith, and other gifts—for God wants to give no one the Spirit or faith outside of the outward word and the signs instituted by him; and (5) he comes to us in the word, the sacraments, and the keys in order to remind his people that they are the true church.

As God works in history, he is disguised and concealed, as a man may hide behind a mask. The history of the nations is the history of an active God who uses the nations as his delegates to destroy other, godless nations as his agents of wrath. Nations do not perish of themselves but God wipes them out because of their sins. Hence, history is the stage upon which God executes his judgments and the stage in which he works his salvation.

Moreover, God has ordained temporal and spiritual government as the two means by which he rules the world; and for the individual, they are the two different ways in which a person encounters the divine reality. Spiritual government is to give its life in the proclamation of the gospel and the salvation of souls; and temporal government is to give its life for the temporal well-being of humankind.

In God's ordered power of the church, home, and government, God seeks to govern his world for humankind's good and to reveal, in a daily fashion, his care toward all people. In these three orders, it is his will that we perceive the Father's face as others patiently rule over us. Through these ordered powers, he desires to be graciously seen and known as he works through his creatures and accomplishes his purposes and will in the world.

Thus God clothes himself in the form of a human person who performs his work on earth. Through vocation the person serves as a mask of God behind which he can conceal himself as he pours out his gifts into our lives, and our only care ought to be what should I do with all the good gifts that God has given me so that it may benefit my neighbor.

Just as faith constitutes the proper relationship of a believer to God, so good works and love exercised in vocation define a person's relationship to one's neighbor; because a Christian lives and labors on earth, not for oneself, but for one's neighbor. All Christian life can be summed up in two words: faith and love; whereby the believer is placed midway between God and one's neighbor, receiving from above and giving out below, and becoming his instrument through which his divine goodness flows into the life of one's neighbor.

Chapter 2: God's Word and Work: The Ministry of the Word, the Will of His Good Pleasure, and the Will of the Sign

From the very beginning of human history, through the ministry of the word, God has spoken to human beings through the instrumentality of men and angels. Moreover, if you divide all Scripture, as it pertains to the ministry of the word, it contains two topics:

threats and promises.[1] Consequently, wrote Luther, "this does concern me, that I know what He has commanded, what He has promised, and what He has threatened. When you reflect on these things, you find God, yes, He Himself takes you on His lap."[2]

After Adam and Eve had sinned (Gen 3:1–24), the Father revealed his heart and pointed to a deliverance through the seed of a woman. It is through the "will of His good pleasure," observed Luther, that we are able to look into the very heart and will of the Father; and there we see that God is compassionate and does not desire the death of the sinner, but that the sinner should have eternal life.[3]

In his incarnation, God himself would be present yet hidden and concealed. In Christ, God is found, and outside the person born of Mary he is not to be found. Therefore, the person who encounters this flesh encounters God. Moreover, it is the purpose of his concealment that he can be seen, touched, and apprehended without the beholder being consumed by his majesty. If a person is to meet God, he or she must come to Christ; for his incarnation is the only view of the Divinity permitted and possible in this life. Yet his presence can be seen, and apprehended, only by faith; for it is only by faith, acquired through the word, that a person can cut through the coverings of flesh and blood and see him in his incarnation.

After the fall of Adam and Eve into sin, God, in the sacrifices, willed that some outward and visible sign of his grace be placed alongside the word so that human beings might be reminded of his mercy and would believe with greater assurance that he is kind and merciful. In this sign, Adam and Eve could perceive that they had not been cast off by God but that they were still the object of God's concern and regard.

1. Luther, *Luther's Works*, 3:225. "When God makes a promise, there He Himself is dealing with us and is giving and offering us something. But when He gives a command through the law, He is requiring something from us, and He wants us to do something" (Luther, *Luther's Works*, 3:24).

2. Luther, *Luther's Works*, 3:139.

3. John 3:16–17.

Later, circumcision was enjoined upon Abraham in order that it might be a sacrament through which his descendants would be made righteous if they believed the promise that the Lord attached to it. But circumcision was more: it was a sign to the nations that the promised Savior would be born from this circumcised nation. In this way, God has always provided some public sign whereby the nations might find the true God.

In our human weakness and comprehension, we are in need of such signs so that we might find him but also so that we do not seek him in some other way. Thus, prior to circumcision, the ministry of the word and the sacrifices were visible signs of the invisible grace; but circumcision, which was instituted under Abraham, had validity up to the coming of the Blessed Seed. Since the coming of Christ, God continues to speak to us in a fatherly manner through the ministry of the word and his sacraments; these signs, along with the word, are our light bearers today and wherever these are, there we find Christ, the forgiveness of sins, and eternal life.

Chapter 3: The True and False Church

God and Satan, since the garden of Eden, have been engaged in a great conflict for the soul of every human being. God wants every person to be saved and Satan wants every person to perish eternally. Moreover, the world and its god (Satan) cannot and will not bear the word of the true God to be made known, and the true God cannot and will not keep silent.

As a result of this conflict, two kinds of people are derived from the two sons born to Adam. The whole course of history is the intermingling of two peoples, going back as far as Abel and Cain. It is with Adam, Eve, and their offspring that we see that two generations of human beings are being dealt with: the one of the righteous, which is the true church; the other of the unrighteous, which is the false church. Therefore, from the beginning, there is a twofold church in the world just as the seed is twofold.

It is with the sacrifices of Abel and Cain that we begin to differentiate between the true and false church. Cain appears to be saintly but he is ungodly and does not believe the divine promise concerning the Blessed Seed. Abel, on the other hand, by faith took hold of the promise given to Adam concerning the Seed; and this faith is the reason why he offered a better sacrifice than Cain. Therefore the true church is made up of those who have the promise and believe it. The false church does not believe these promises of God and concerns itself with things that he has not commanded nor promised.

Moreover, wherever the word is, there Satan is active and seeks to spread false teaching by corrupting the word of God in such a way that human beings doubt the goodness of God. The pattern of Satan's temptations are all the same; he first puts faith to trial and draws people away from the word to have them listen to another word. Therefore the person who wants to deal with God must learn that a person does not live by bread alone but by every word that proceeds from the mouth of God; for the kingdom of God is a kingdom of the word, as he calls and rules his people by the word alone.

Chapter 4: God's Way of Governing His People

This is the history of the saints, as witnessed in the lives of Noah, Abraham, Jacob, and Joseph: that they hear the word, believe it, and are exercised in faith by many tribulations. They learned that in the darkness of the cross and the trial, they were to cling to the word of God alone. Yet this knowledge of God, and his way of governing their lives, did not come without practice and experience. These things were done by God so that they might learn what is the good, acceptable, and perfect will of God and be equipped to comfort others in their trials.

The general rule is that God makes his saints sad again after they have been gladdened, and that one should look for comfort after tribulation and tribulation after comfort. Moreover, as God leads his saints, one trial immediately follows another, compelling the believer to exercise faith and to engage in a life of frequent prayer and praise. Just as trials drive us to prayer and faith, so, when the saints are delivered, they are impelled to give thanks and praise to God for his mercy.

For when we are not subjected to trials, observed Luther, Christians forget their spiritual exercises; and, without a trial, we learn nothing and make no progress. Therefore God sends trials in order that from day to day we may understand and cling to the promises of God more clearly and certainly.

Thus God's testing is a fatherly one. He does not test in order that we may fear and hate him like a tyrant but to the end that he may exercise and stir up faith and love in us. Satan, however, tempts for evil in order to draw you away from God and to make you distrust and blaspheme God. Moreover, if the devil notices that you have the word and are confident that your life is pleasing and acceptable to God on account of the word, he will not rest but will put in your way trials and afflictions of every kind.

In trials we learn patience, faith, and hope; for this is how God exercises, exalts, and plays with his saints. It is out of his great love for us that he works in our lives in this manner. "For these exercises are useful to this end, that we learn to understand the mercy[4] of God, and the mystery of faith and hope, and in some manner comprehend the inscrutable plans of God concerning us."[5]

Chapter 5: A Series of Theses Concerning the Masks of God and How God Governs His People

The chapter extracts and formulates selected theses from the text and footnotes shared in chapters 1 through 4 as a means for review, reflection, edification, and conversation.

4. For "the Scriptures reveal that even the greatest heroes of the church were human beings, that is, they often fell, often sinned, and nevertheless were received back into grace by a merciful God. So these examples are useful both to instill the fear of God into hearts and to sustain faith or trust in mercy" (Luther, *Luther's Works*, 2:240).

5. Luther, *Luther's Works*, 6:354.

Chapter 6: How Do I Find a Gracious God? And Other Questions of the Heart

The final chapter explores several existential questions[6] and subjects in light of the human condition and considers how Luther's understanding of the masks of God provides an evangelical response.

6. "How do I find a gracious God?"; "Are you the only one who knows anything? Except for you is all the church in error?"; "Father, if Jesus exists, how come he never lives here?"

CHAPTER 1

The Masks of God

Introduction to the Masks of God

"MAN SHALL NOT SEE me and live" (Exod 33:20). As a result of our sinful nature human beings cannot see God, in his naked transcendence, and survive. Therefore, since the fall of humankind into sin, there can be no unmediated relationship between God and human beings. God must wear a mask in all of his dealings with us.

Moreover, Luther held that this nature[1] of ours has become so misshapen through sin that it cannot recognize God[2] nor comprehend his nature[3] without a covering. Therefore God, in his grace

1. "Our nature is so corrupt that it no longer knows God unless it is enlightened by the Word and the Spirit of God" (Luther, *Luther's Works*, 2:124).

2. "Thus all men naturally understand and come to the conclusion that God is some kind of beneficent divine power, from whom all good things are to be sought and hoped for . . . even though they err in the Person of God because of idolatry, the devotion which is owed to the true God is nevertheless there, that is, invocation and the expectation of blessings and help" (Luther, *Luther's Works*, 6:113).

3. "It is folly to argue much about God outside and before time, because this is an effort to understand the Godhead without a covering, or the uncovered divine essence" (Luther, *Luther's Works*, 1:11). God dwells in unapproachable light and "we cannot define what God is in His nature" (Luther, *Luther's Works*, 2:46). Thus, "God, in His essence, is incomprehensible and dwells in a light which we cannot approach . . . therefore we must stay with the Word" (Luther, *Luther's Works*, 3:138).

and mercy, envelops himself in his word and works and seeks to reveal himself to us in certain forms.

> Let no one, therefore, contemplate the unveiled Divinity,[4] but let him flee from these contemplations as from hell and the veritable temptations of Satan. Let it be the concern of each of us to abide by the signs by which God has revealed Himself to us, namely, His Son, born of the virgin Mary and lying in His manger among the cattle; the Word; Baptism; the Lord's Supper; and absolution. In these images we see and meet a God whom we can bear, One who comforts us, lifts us up into hope, and saves us.[5]

Since it is impossible to know God in his uncovered essence[6] it would be most unwise, warned Luther, to argue about God and the divine nature without the word or any covering.[7] Those who seek to reach God apart from these coverings[8] exert to ascend into

4. "It is the true contemplative life to hear and believe the spoken Word and to want to know nothing except Christ and Him crucified. He alone, with His Word, is the profitable and salutary object of contemplation" (Luther, *Luther's Works*, 3:276).

5. Luther, *Luther's Works*, 2:48.

6. "Concerning these matters we cannot establish or think out anything, because outside that beginning of the creation there is nothing except the uncovered divine essence and the uncovered God" (Luther, *Luther's Works*, 1:17–18). "God in His essence is altogether unknowable; nor is it possible to define or put into words what He is. . . . It is for this reason that God lowers Himself to the level of our weak comprehension and presents Himself to us in images, in coverings, as it were, in simplicity adapted to a child, that in some measure it may be possible for Him to be known by us" (Luther, *Luther's Works*, 2:45).

7. "For it is certain that a human being cannot find God through his own wisdom . . . we shall be safe from these dangers if we follow that visible form or those signs which God Himself set before us" (Luther, *Luther's Works*, 3:108–9). "In the New Testament we have as a visible form the Son of God on the lap of His mother Mary . . . besides, we have other visible forms: Baptism, the Eucharist, and the spoken Word itself" (Luther, *Luther's Works*, 3:109).

8. "Christ must be sought where He has manifested Himself and wants to be known, as in the Word, in Baptism, and in the Supper; there He is certainly found" (Luther, *Luther's Works*, 3:108). "For we have need of marks and signs of this kind, in order that they may lead us to the knowledge of God, since human reason is unable to find God unless such signs instituted by God lead

heaven without ladders, that is, without the only true Ladder who is Jesus Christ.

The Concrete Spirit

> But you must adhere to and follow this sure and infallible rule: God in His divine wisdom arranges to manifest Himself to human beings by some definite and visible form which can be seen by the eyes and touched with the hands, in short, is within the scope of the five senses. So near to us does the Divine Majesty place Itself.[9]

The Holy Spirit's ministry is thoroughly external[10] and completely available to our senses. God could have saved the human race[11] in another way, but it is his will to save fallen humankind through external means and to reveal himself to us in this way. It is in these forms that the Holy Spirit is clearly exhibited to our eyes.

Since the Holy Spirit works nothing without externals, it is the responsibility of every human being to apprehend him where and in what manner he has chosen to make himself known. It is only in Christ, and in the forms instituted by him, that God reveals himself to us. They are the God-given means of knowing God; and they are the places where he is present for us. Luther offers five reasons why God comes to us through his concrete Spirit:

---

us by the hand, so to speak. And nothing is more dangerous than if one devises his own way to God and relies on his own speculations" (Luther, *Luther's Works*, 3:107).

9. Luther, *Luther's Works*, 3:109.

10. "It is indeed true that the Holy Spirit alone enlightens hearts and kindles faith, but He does not do this without the outward ministry and without the outward use of the sacraments" (Luther, *Luther's Works*, 4:72).

11. "By His almighty power God could save the human race without Christ, without Baptism, and without the Word of the Gospel. He could have illuminated men's hearts inwardly through the Holy Spirit and forgiven their sins without the ministry of the Word and of ministers. But it was not His will to do so" (Luther, *Luther's Works*, 6:128).

First, since the beginning of the world,[12] divine wisdom has so ordained and arranged things that there is always some public sign[13] toward which all people might look in order that they might find,[14] worship, and pray to the true God and be saved.[15]

Second, these outward and visible signs[16] have been placed alongside the word so that human beings, "reminded by the outward sign and work or Sacrament, would believe with greater assurance that God is kind and merciful."[17] By means of these visible

12. "In order to reinforce the promise of our salvation, God had this in mind from the very beginning of the world: men were to have signs by means of which they might comfort themselves in their sins and gain courage through their reliance on divine grace" (Luther, *Luther's Works*, 1:250). "The doctrine of the Gospel has been in the world ever since the first parents fell, and by various signs God confirmed this promise to the fathers. The earlier times know nothing of the rainbow, circumcision, and other things that were ordained later on. But all ages had the knowledge of the Blessed Seed" (Luther, *Luther's Works*, 2:163–64).

13. "Therefore it is great praise of God's mercy that He did not let the human race walk and go astray in its own thoughts but set up for those who feared Him public signs at which they might gather" (Luther, *Luther's Works*, 3:145).

14. "Thus the church has never been deprived to such an extent of outward signs that it became impossible to know where God could surely be found" (Luther, *Luther's Works*, 1:248).

15. "Whoever desires to be saved and to be safe when he deals with such great matters, let him simply hold to the form, the signs, and the coverings of the Godhead, such as His Word and His works. For in His Word and in His works He shows Himself to us" (Luther, *Luther's Works*, 1:13).

16. "This doubt [whether you were in grace or not] Christ wanted to remove from us not only by His Word but also by these visible signs of grace. Therefore He added such clear promises to these signs—promises that are applied to the individuals when they make use of these signs" (Luther, *Luther's Works*, 3:124). For God did not come down from heaven to make you uncertain but He instituted the sacraments, absolution, etc. to make you completely certain and "to remove the disease of doubt from your heart, in order that you not only believe with the heart but also see with our physical eyes and touch with your hands" (Luther, *Luther's Works*, 5:45).

17. "Our merciful God always placed some outward and visible sign of His grace alongside the Word, so that men, reminded by the outward sign and work or Sacrament, would believe with greater assurance that God is kind and merciful" (Luther, *Luther's Works*, 1:248).

signs of grace, God shows us that he is with us, takes care of us, and is favorably inclined toward us.

> I have always displayed Myself to the eyes and ears of men in such a way that they could become aware of My presence in the sacrifices, in circumcision, in burning incense, in the cloud, in the Red Sea, in the manna, in the brazen serpent, in the tabernacle of Moses, in the temple of Solomon, and in the cloud. And it was My delight to display and reveal Myself in this manner to the children of men. . . . In the same way the very Word, Baptism, and the Eucharist are our lightbearers today, toward which we look as dependable tokens of the sun of grace. We can state with certainty that where the Eucharist, Baptism, and the Word are, there are Christ, forgiveness of sins, and eternal life.[18]

Third, he presents himself to us in these visible forms in order that we might be kept from degenerating into the erratic and vagabond spirits who boast of visions and revelations and follow them.[19] Since we cannot ascend to him, he has chosen to come to us and reveal himself within the range of our comprehension so that he can be found and known. The true God is not a wandering God but has limited himself to a certain place[20] and certain external forms. As God has provided reliable, concrete marks of

18. Luther, *Luther's Works*, 1:248–49.

19. "He presents Himself to us in these visible forms, deals with us, and puts these forms before us to keep us from degenerating into erratic and vagabond spirits who indeed carry on discussions about God but are profoundly ignorant of Him as of One who cannot be comprehended in His unveiled majesty" (Luther, *Luther's Works*, 2:46).

20. For Moses and God's people during their wilderness journey, God designated "for them a definite place and calls it the Tabernacle, that is, the appointed, definite and fixed place. This tabernacle God gave to Moses as a sure sign of the place He had chosen, and He added the promise that He would dwell there, be present, and hear the invocations and prayers of those who call upon Him" (Luther, *Luther's Works*, 4:178). In the New Testament period, "God calls us back to the place where the memory of His name is, to our tabernacle, which is the ministry of the Word. Where the Word resounds and the sacraments are administered according to Christ's institution, this is the true tabernacle of God" (Luther, *Luther's Works*, 4:179).

his presence, so it is the mark of all false spirits to cast aside the external word and signs and to tell God how he must deal with them.[21]

Fourth, as God comes to us in these concrete forms, he deals with us in a twofold manner, first outwardly, then inwardly. He draws us outwardly through Christ's word and the gospel and inwardly through the Holy Spirit. Outwardly[22] he deals with us through the oral word of the gospel and through materials signs; inwardly, he deals with us through the Holy Spirit, faith, and other gifts. Thus

> the inward experience follows and is effected by the outward. God has determined to give the inward to no one except through the outward. For He wants to give no one the Spirit or faith outside of the outward Word and sign instituted by Him. . . . Observe carefully, my brother, this order, for everything depends on it.[23]

Fifth, he comes to us in the word, the sacraments, and the keys[24] in order to prepare us for his second coming and to remind his people that, until he comes, they are the true church.

21. "They disdain to hear from Him how they are to find Him; but they presume to teach, and to prescribe to, Him how He should deal with them. But God will not submit to this; for He is not the man to be ordered about and to institute something particular for each individual or to issue a new Gospel, a new Baptism, message, or revelation for your sake. Once and for all He has ordained and proclaimed this concerning Christ: Here is the Man whom you must hear if you want to come to Me and be saved. I herewith serve notice on you that I will give you no other sign. Therefore mark well that you must either accept Him or be lost." (Luther, *Luther's Works*, 24:69).

22. "God, who manifests and reveals Himself to us in order that we may learn to know Him. This is the first principle and the foundation that is set forth in all Scripture. First of all . . . something, either a word or deed, must precede which moves us, and this first impulse must be from God . . . we hear God speaking the Word, and we feel Him working through the oral Word and the sacraments, through which He awakens in us knowledge of Him" (Luther, *Luther's Works*, 5:258).

23. Luther, *Luther's Works*, 40:146.

24. The office of the keys is that special authority that Christ has given to his church on earth to forgive the sins of repentant sinners, but to withhold forgiveness from the unrepentant as long as they do not repent.

Thus, in order that God might be known and comprehended, the Spirit of Christ meets us in simple, earthly, and concrete ways. These concrete forms of the Holy Spirit are God's way to us and are a rejection of every way from man to God. These are the common epiphanies or appearances for all people.[25] When God comes to us, he does not hide himself in a corner but appears publicly before us all. When we get to heaven we shall see God differently, but here we see him enveloped in his word and sacraments. These are, and will remain, his masks, until the day of judgment.

History as a Mask of God

History is the account of God exalting those of low degree and putting down the mighty[26] as he sends one nation against another nation. Thus, the history of the nations is the history of the active God who uses the nations as his delegates to destroy other, godless nations as his agents of wrath.[27]

> We see in all histories and in experiences that He puts down one kingdom and exalts another, lifts up one principality and casts down another, increases one people and destroys another; as He did with Assyria, Babylon, Persia, Greece and Rome, though they thought they should sit on their seats forever.[28]

Thus, the historical process moves along these interpretive lines. God allows the ungodly to become great and mighty[29] to

25. Luther, *Luther's Works*, 3:168.

26. "It is profitable to observe and note such examples diligently. They are intended to frighten the proud and to humble us, that we may learn that our lives and all that we have depend on God's approval, who is disposed to give grace to the humble but to destroy the proud" (Luther, *Luther's Works*, 2:4).

27. "Wrath is truly God's alien work, in which He engages contrary to His nature, because He is forced into it by the wickedness of man" (Luther, *Luther's Works*, 2:134).

28. Luther, *Luther's Works*, 21:344.

29. "Ungodly government are like God's swine. He fattens them; He gives them wealth, power, honors, and the obedience of their subjects. Therefore they are not molested, but they themselves molest and oppress others. They do

exalt themselves. Then he withdraws his power from them and lets them puff themselves up in their own power alone. When their bubble is full blown, and they themselves feel safe and secure, then God plucks the bubble and all is over. They do not even know that while they are puffing themselves up and growing strong they are forsaken of God and God's arm is not with them; and when their iniquities have been filled up, God withdraws his hand. Nations do not perish of themselves but God wipes them out because of their sins.

Hence, history is the stage upon which God executes his judgments and the stage in which he works his salvation. As God works in history, he is disguised and concealed, as a man may hide behind a mask; yet all events in history, all persons in history, and all forces in history are masks of God, who works all in all.

Temporal and Spiritual Government

The children of Adam and all of humankind can be divided into two classes, the first belonging to the kingdom of God[30] and the second to the kingdom of the world.[31] For this reason God has ordained two governments: spiritual government is to give its life in the proclamation of the gospel and the salvation of souls; and

not suffer violence, but they inflict it on others. They do not give, but they take away from others until the hour when they are slaughtered like swine that have been fattened for a long time" (Luther, *Luther's Works*, 2:35–36).

30. "Those who belong to the kingdom of God are all the true believers who are in Christ and under Christ, for Christ is the King and Lord in the kingdom of God" (Luther, *Luther's Works*, 45:88). They need no temporal law or sword "since Christians have in their heart the Holy Spirit, who both teaches and makes them to do injustice to no one, to love everyone, and to suffer injustice and even death willingly and cheerfully at the hands of anyone" (Luther, *Luther's Works*, 45:89).

31. "All who are not Christians belong to the kingdom of the world and are under the law . . . [and God] has subjected them to the sword so that, even though they would like to, they are unable to practice their wickedness, and if they do practice it, they cannot do so without fear" (Luther, *Luther's Works*, 45:90).

temporal government is to give its life for the temporal well-being of humankind.[32]

These two governments stand to each other as the right and left hand of God respectively; and they constitute the two means by which God rules the world. For the individual, they are two different ways in which a person encounters the divine reality.

> For God has established two governments among men. The one is spiritual; it has no sword, but it has the word,[33] by means of which men are to become good and righteous, so that with this righteousness they may attain eternal life. He administers this righteousness through the word, which He has committed to preachers. The other kind is worldly government,[34] which works through the sword[35] so that those who do not want to be good and righteous to eternal life may be forced to become good and righteous in the eyes of the world. He administers this righteousness through the sword.[36]

Therefore, as long as the world endures, both governments are to remain: spiritual government is to proclaim an evangelical righteousness and temporal government is to bring about external peace and restrain and punish evil deeds. Moreover, neither

32. In temporal government he grants earthly gifts and cares for the temporal well-being of humankind.

33. "Christians can be ruled by nothing except God's word, for Christians must be ruled in faith . . . [for] faith can come through no word of man, but only through the Word of God" (Luther, *Luther's Works*, 45:117).

34. God has made temporal government subject to reason and law because it has nothing to do with the salvation of souls; therefore the wisdom of the Greek and Roman poets, historians, and jurists can be used in promoting order. Moreover, temporal government is more than political authorities and governments; it includes everything that contributes to the preservation of this earthly life.

35. "It is God's will that the temporal sword and law be used for the punishment of the wicked and the protection of the upright" (Luther, *Luther's Works*, 45:87). "Those who do not believe are not Christians; they do not belong to Christ's kingdom, but to the worldly kingdom where they are constrained and governed by the sword and by outward rule" (Luther, *Luther's Works*, 45:118).

36. Luther, *Luther's Works*, 46:99.

government is sufficient in the world without the other.[37] For example, if anyone attempted to rule the entire country or the world by the gospel, it

> would be like a shepherd who should put together in one fold wolves, lions, eagles, and sheep, and let them mingle freely with one another, saying, "Help yourselves, be good and peaceful toward one another. The fold is open, there is plenty of food. You need have no fear of dogs or clubs." The sheep would doubtless keep the peace and allow themselves to be fed and governed peacefully, but they would not live long, nor would one beast survive another.[38]

Furthermore, each government is to remain within its sphere of ministry. For example, the temporal government has laws that extend no further than to life and property and external affairs on earth, for God cannot and will not permit anyone but himself to rule over the soul.[39] Therefore, whenever the temporal government prescribes laws for the soul, it encroaches upon God's government. Consequently,

> Since a true Christian lives and labors on earth not for himself alone but for his neighbor[40]. . . [and] because the sword is most beneficial and necessary for the whole world in order to preserve peace, punish sin, and restrain the wicked, the Christian submits most willingly to the rule of the sword, pays his taxes, honors those in

37. Luther, *Luther's Works*, 45:92. "No one can become righteous in the sight of God by means of the temporal government, without Christ's spiritual government . . . for without the Holy Spirit in the heart no one becomes truly righteous . . . on the other hand, where the spiritual government alone prevails over land and people, there wickedness is given free rein and the door is open for all manner of rascality" (Luther, *Luther's Works*, 45:92).

38. Luther, *Luther's Works*, 45:92.

39. Luther, *Luther's Works*, 45:105. "The soul is not under the authority of Caesar" (Luther, *Luther's Works*, 45:111).

40. "All Christians have been placed into the world for the purpose of serving their neighbors, not only so far as the Second Table is concerned but rather so far as the First Table is concerned, in order that they may learn to fear God and to trust in His mercy" (Luther, *Luther's Works*, 3:240).

> authority, serves, helps, and does all he can to assist the governing authority that it may continue to function and be held in honor and fear.[41]

God's Ordered Power[42]

Luther, in his explanation as to why God limits himself through external means, speaks of his ordered power.[43] God could save and work without externals and order, but it is his will to limit[44] his power as he works among us. He does this so that, as he works through his created orders of church, home, and government, his creatures have opportunity to share in his work. In these three orders,[45] God seeks to govern[46] his world for humankind's good and to reveal, in a daily fashion, his care toward all of humankind.

41. Luther, *Luther's Works*, 45:94.

42. God's ordered power is "when He makes use of the service of either angels or of human beings" (Luther, *Luther's Works*, 3:274). "For God wants to govern the world through angels and through human beings, His creatures, as through His servants, just as He gives light through the sun, the moon, and even through fire and candles" (Luther, *Luther's Works*, 3:273).

43. "God no longer wants to act in accordance with His extraordinary or absolute power . . . but wants to act through His creatures, whom He does not want to be idle" (Luther, *Luther's Works*, 3:274). For God rules us in such a way that he does not want us to be idle: "He gives us food and clothing, but in such a way that we should plow, sow, reap and cook. In addition, He gives offspring, which is born and grows because of the blessing of God and must nevertheless be cherished, cared for, brought up, and instructed by parents" (Luther, *Luther's Works*, 8:94).

44. An example of God's absolute power took place in Babylon when Daniel's companions continued to live unharmed (Dan 3:25) in the midst of the fire (Luther, *Luther's Works*, 3:274).

45. "This life is profitably divided into three orders: (1) life in the home; (2) life in the state; and (3) life in the church" (Luther, *Luther's Works*, 3:217). In and through these orders, God seeks to protect "the human race against the devil, the flesh, and the world" (Luther, *Luther's Works*, 3:279).

46. "God has appointed three social classes to which He has given the command not to let sins go unpunished. The first is that of the parents, who should maintain strict discipline in their house when ruling the domestics and the children. The second is the government, for the officers of the state bear

The Church

The first ordered power established by God was the church and, by its primacy,[47] God desired human beings to know that they were created for immortality and eternal life with God. Adam, in his unspoiled human nature, would have lived for a definite time in paradise, according to God's pleasure, then he would have been carried off to that rest of God.

After the fall, and in order to grant people eternal life and salvation, God willed to reveal himself through the ordered power of his word and the various signs placed alongside the word. Therefore, wherever the word and the visible signs are, there the church is established; for the church exists only where the word is.

Also, size does not make the church; since those who keep the word are the church even though they are very few in number. Consequently, exclaimed Luther, "if I were the only one in the entire world to adhere to the Word, I alone would be the church."[48]

Therefore God, in order to accomplish his ministry of bringing comfort to wounded consciences, and leading people into the kingdom of heaven, "has always preserved for Himself a people who would cling to the Word and be the guardian of religion and of sound doctrine in the world."[49]

Luther identified three primary characteristics of the church. First, the church is the pupil of Christ; they are a people who sit at his feet and who listen to his word so that they may know how

---

the sword for the purpose of coercing the obstinate and remiss by means of their power of discipline. The third is that of the church, which governs by the Word. By this threefold authority God has protected the human race against the devil, the flesh, and the world, to the end that offenses may not increase but may be cut off" (Luther, *Luther's Works*, 3:279).

47. "Here we have the establishment of the church before there was any government of the home and of the state; for Eve was not yet created. Moreover, the church is established without walls and without any pomp, in a very spacious and very delightful place" (Luther, *Luther's Works*, 1:103).

48. Luther, *Luther's Works*, 2:102.

49. Luther, *Luther's Works*, 2:228–29.

to judge all things.[50] As the pupil of Christ, the church does not teach anything except what has been entrusted to it by Christ.[51] Second, the church is also the lodging place in which the people who feel sin, death, and the terrors and vexations of an afflicted and wounded conscience are healed.[52] Third, the church serves as the house of God that leads from earth to heaven.[53]

The Home

After the church was established, God brought the ordered power of the home into existence. The household was set up when God made a husband of lonely Adam and joined him to a wife as his companion[54] and to bring about the increase of the human race. Marriage is the divinely instituted and lawful union of a man and a woman,[55] not only according to the law of nature but also according to God's will. Foremost, it is "a lawful union not only of bodies but also of hearts."[56]

Thus, marriage "is the first and chief thing; for it is the beginning and origin of the whole life."[57] Even though God is able to

50. Luther, *Luther's Works*, 2:353.

51. Luther, *Luther's Works*, 2:356.

52. Luther, *Luther's Works*, 8:54.

53. "This, then, is the complete definition of the church, which is the habitation of God on earth. Not that we should remain on earth, but the sacraments are administered and the Word is taught in order that we may be led into the kingdom of heaven and through the church may enter into heaven" (Luther, *Luther's Works*, 5:250).

54. "After the church has been established, the household government is also set up, when Eve is added to Adam as his companion" (Luther, *Luther's Works*, 1:103).

55. Luther, *Luther's Works*, 4:244.

56. "The world does not understand this but dreams that marriage is nothing else than sexual intercourse, kisses and embraces. But it is a lawful union not only of bodies but also of hearts" (Luther, *Luther's Works*, 5:32).

57. Luther, *Luther's Works*, 5:189. Marriage "is the source and origin of the household, the state and the church" (Luther, *Luther's Works*, 4:249).

make a human being out of clay,[58] God wills to make use of the union of male and female to bestow the blessing of life.

After a husband and wife have been united in this married life, "they plan and work together, provide food for themselves and their children, bring up their children in the fear of God, and rule the household."[59] For its ultimate purpose

> is to obey God and to be remedy[60] for sin; to call upon God; to desire, love, and bring up children to the glory of God; to live with one's spouse in the fear of the Lord; and to bear one's cross. But if no children result, you should nevertheless live with your spouse and avoid promiscuity.[61]

In the management of the household, father and mother are the instruments through which God seeks to form citizens for the state but, most importantly, for the kingdom of Christ and heaven. Therefore, marriage should be treated with honor;[62] from it we all

58. "Furthermore, He no longer wants to form human beings from a clod, as He formed Adam, but He makes use of the union of a male and a female, on whom He bestows His blessing" (Luther, *Luther's Works*, 3:274).

59. Luther, *Luther's Works*, 3:48.

60. "Marriage is necessary as a remedy for lust, and through marriage God permits sexual intercourse. Not only does He cover the sin from which we are unable to abstain, but He also blesses the union of the male and the female. And yet the whole world shuns this legitimate, divinely instituted union and prefers to indulge in promiscuous relations, which are harmful in more than one way. Property is squandered, bodies are damaged by serious diseases, God is provoked to inflict horrible punishments, and, worst of all, states and households are destroyed" (Luther, *Luther's Works*, 3:48).

61. Luther, *Luther's Works*, 4:244. "But if you cannot avoid being joined to a woman without sinning, use the remedy shown by God. And if you do not seek the function of bringing children into being, at least seek the remedy against sin, in order that fornication and adultery may be avoided as well as pollutions and promiscuous lusts" (Luther, *Luther's Works*, 5:190).

62. "God did not institute marriage for the sake of lust and the pleasures of the flesh. This is not the final cause, but marriage serves a twofold purpose: in the first place, to be a remedy against lust; in the second place, to be a source and origin of the human race, in order that offspring may be born and the human race may be propagated" (Luther, *Luther's Works*, 5:189). "But from the Holy Scripture one should add the purpose of bringing up children in the

originate, and "it is the nursery not only for the state but also for the church and the kingdom of Christ until the end of the world."[63]

Government

Finally, it was not until the entry of sin into the world that civil government, God's third ordered power, was established. God, in his wisdom, foresaw[64] that there would be a great abundance of evil people in the world and that an outward remedy would be required to hold sin in check; for this is the one and foremost function of government.[65]

Government is God's rod and sword, a minister of his wrath[66] in order to punish all sins forbidden in the second table.[67] Yet, it takes no pleasure in such punishments for it would prefer to have everyone do his duty and not to deserve punishment at all.[68] Hence the most important duties of government are to uphold the law, to maintain peace, and to preserve justice.

---

discipline and fear of the Lord in order that they may be equipped to govern the church and the state" (Luther, *Luther's Works*, 5:189).

63. Luther, *Luther's Works*, 1:240.

64. "Because He foresaw that there would always be a great abundance of evil men, He established an outward remedy . . . with this hedge, these walls, God has given protection for our life and possessions" (Luther, *Luther's Works*, 2:141).

65. "There was no government of the state before sin, for there was no need of it. Civil government is a remedy required by our corrupted nature. It is necessary that lust be held in check by the bonds of the law and by penalties" (Luther, *Luther's Works*, 1:104).

66. Governments "are the masks of wrath against the wicked and a source of comfort for the good and oppressed" (Luther, *Luther's Works*, 7:191).

67. "In short, it should punish all sins forbidden in the Second Table" (Luther, *Luther's Works*, 2:141).

68. Luther, *Luther's Works*, 7:254.

In this ordered power of government, God wills to share his power[69] with human beings and grants them power[70] over life and death[71] in order that the essentials of life might be preserved and ensured. Moreover, reasoned Luther, "if God grants to man power over life and death, surely He also grants power over what is less, such as property, the home, spouse, children, servants and fields."[72]

Thus, observed Luther, a good term for government is to call them saviors[73] or healers, who cure the abscesses and ailments of the body, put thieves and robbers to death, and defend their people against acts of violence through holy justice.[74] For God wants evildoers to be condemned and the godly defended. Without these masks, peace and discipline could not be preserved. Therefore,

69. Before the flood, God reserved all judgment for himself and did not permit one human being to kill another human being, as the examples of Cain and Lamech show. After the flood, God shares his power over life and death with man provided that the person is guilty of shedding blood. For "human beings have the power to kill only when we are guilty before the world and when the crime has been established. For this reason courts have been established and a definite method of procedure has been prescribed. Thus a crime must be investigated and proved before the death sentence is imposed" (Luther, *Luther's Works*, 2:140).

70. "Whosoever sheds the blood of man, by man shall his blood be shed" (Gen 9:6). "But the life of one who does not want to show respect for the image of God in man but wants to yield to his anger . . . this life God turns over to government in order that this life, too, may be shed" (Luther, *Luther's Works*, 2:141).

71. "Here the executioner must wield the sword and make use of the gallows in order to frighten and warn the others, even when the sin is forgiven. Thus although the thief is pardoned, nevertheless he is brought to the gallows. The sin of those who suffer capital punishment is forgiven by God but the executioner does not forgive it" (Luther, *Luther's Works*, 8:205). "The magistrate, therefore, kills not by virtue of the Second Table, but by virtue of the First Table, nor is his killing unjust, although it is really homicide" (Luther, *Luther's Works*, 6:29). "The vengeance of the magistrate is murder in the Second Table; in the First Table it is justice" (Luther, *Luther's Works*, 6:30).

72. Luther, *Luther's Works*, 2:140.

73. Luther, *Luther's Works*, 2:366.

74. "They say that as often as Emperor Maximilian passed by a place of public execution, he uncovered his head and saluted it with these words: Hail, holy justice!" (Luther, *Luther's Works*, 8:205).

those who serve in government[75] should reflect on the fear of God and humble themselves before him as they govern and serve those under their care.

In these three orders, it is God's will that we perceive a fatherly face[76] as others patiently rule over us. Through his ordered power, he desires to be graciously seen and known as he works all things through his creatures[77] and accomplishes his purposes and will in the world.

Vocation: The Link Between Heaven and Earth

Every Christian occupies a number of offices and positions at the same time. For example, a person might be a father, husband, and employee. As he works within his office, he participates in God's own care for human beings. God pours out his gifts into our lives, and our only care ought to be what we should do with all the good that God has made so that it may benefit our neighbor.

Thus God clothes himself in the form of an ordinary person who performs his work on earth. Through vocation the person

75. Those who serve in government "should be taught and learn what God is and what He does through the government and the rulers, who are the instruments of God's works through which God rules the people. Then they become truly wise and successful in governing" (Luther, *Luther's Works*, 5:122–23).

76. "God's winsome face must be recognized in His promises, in the sacraments, and likewise in external blessings and gifts, in a gracious prince, a neighbor, a father and a mother. When I see that the face of my parents is gracious, I see at the same time the winsome face of God smiling at me" (Luther, *Luther's Works*, 6:173). For example, "as Jacob had previously said that he had seen the Lord face to face, he now discerns the same face of God in the face of his brother Esau, for he sees the good pleasure of God's will in the goodwill and favor of his brother" (Luther, *Luther's Works*, 6:173).

77. "This, then, is the great glory with which the Divine Majesty honors us: It works through us in such a manner that it says that our words are Its words and that our actions are Its actions, so that one can truthfully say that the mouth of a godly teacher is God's mouth and that the hand which you extend to alleviate the want of a brother is God's hand" (Luther, *Luther's Works*, 3:272).

serves as a mask of God behind which he can conceal himself as he scatters his gifts to humankind.

Based upon Eccl. 3:1–17, all human labors and efforts have their fixed time to be started, to be effected, and to be concluded. Therefore the God who moves and commands us to work in our vocation is also the same God who holds the outward course of events in his hands and thus prepares the opportune occasion in which the things commanded are to be accomplished.

Faith Active in Love

Christianity, to Luther, represented a very simple relationship: on the one hand, God's promise; and on the other hand, a believer's faith. "Faith alone lays hold of the promise, believes God when he gives the promise, stretches out its hand when God offers something, and accepts what he offers."[78] Therefore, the only faith that justifies is the faith that deals with God in his promises and accepts them.

Just as faith constitutes the proper relationship of a believer to God, so good works and love exercised in vocation define a person's relationship to his or her neighbor, because Christians live and labor on earth not for themselves, but for their neighbor. Thus, all Christian life can be summed up in two words, faith and love, whereby the believer is placed midway between God and neighbor, receiving from above and giving out below, and becoming his instrument through which his divine goodness flows into the lives of others.

The believer responds to the love of God and plunges into the world as the proper place for the activity and ministry of faith. For

> all Christians have been placed into the world for the purpose of serving our neighbors, not only as far as the Second Table is concerned but rather so far as the First

78. Luther, *Luther's Works*, 3:24.

Table is concerned, in order that they all may learn to fear God and to trust in His mercy.[79]

79. Luther, *Luther's Works*, 3:240.

Chapter 2

God's Word and Work

The Ministry of the Word, the Will of His Good Pleasure, and the Will of the Sign

The Ministry of the Word

From the very beginning of human history, through the ministry of the word, God has spoken to human beings through the instrumentality of men and angels. For example, Luther was pleased with the suggestion that when God confronted Adam with his sin, he spoke through an angel. Through his chronology of the Old Testament, Luther was always able to find a patriarch alive who could speak for God in his place. Adam confronted Cain with the sin of killing his brother as he spoke for God. Methuselah[1] spoke to Noah to enter the ark. Abraham was called by God, through Shem, to leave Ur and go to the promised land. Rebecca consulted Shem or Eber when she was confused about whether or not Jacob should receive the blessing instead of Esau. Finally, Jacob was told to go to Bethel by either Isaac or Deborah. Thus throughout the history of the patriarchs God is speaking, through human beings, his word.

1. Luther believed that it was Methuselah, Noah's grandfather, who told Noah and all his household to go into the ark. "Thus, in my opinion, these words were spoken by Methuselah himself; but they are attributed to God because the Spirit of God spoke through him" (Luther, *Luther's Works*, 2:82).

If you divide all Scripture, as it pertains to the ministry of the word, it contains two topics: threats[2] and promises[3] or law and gospel. Consequently, wrote Luther, "this does concern me, that I know what He has commanded, what He has promised, and what He has threatened."[4]

The Law

The law is the word of God that tells us what we have to do and what judgment we have to expect if we fail to do it. The law was not promulgated for the first time in the Decalogue but is written in the hearts of all people. It is characteristic of the law that its teaching frightens fearful consciences because it does nothing else than teach what God demands from us, what he wants us to do. That is, "it bears witness against us through our conscience, because we have not done the will of God revealed in the Law."[5]

This law demands that you love God with all your heart and your neighbor as yourself. But, observed Luther, "Who, I ask, is there who does this?" Thus God has given the law in order to reveal sin and to work wrath; that is, to announce the wrath of God and punishment to those who sin.

> For the Law is in the heart. It terrifies and is the Law of God . . . accordingly, you are not able to shake off the law; but it shakes your heart, because it is the eternal and

2. "Yet our first and chief care should be the promises and commandments of God, according to which our whole life should be regulated" (Luther, *Luther's Works*, 7:311). "God wants His threats to be feared and His promises to be awaited. But this is impossible without faith" (Luther, *Luther's Works*, 8:202).

3. Luther, *Luther's Works*, 3:225. "When God makes a promise, there He Himself is dealing with us and is giving and offering us something. But when He gives a command through the law, He is requiring something from us, and He wants us to do something" (Luther, *Luther's Works*, 3:24).

4. Luther, *Luther's Works*, 3:139.

5. Luther, *Luther's Works*, 2:158.

> immutable judgment of God, whose accusation and assault you will not easily endure.[6]

The Gospel

The gospel is the word of God that tells us what God has done for us and for our salvation. This doctrine of the gospel has been in the world ever since our first parents fell;[7] and the chief and most important part of the doctrine is the promise. The nature of the promises from God is that "they are given gratis and depend solely on God's mercy, where God alone wants to be the Doer and Worker and demands nothing from us except faith."[8]

> Faith alone lays hold of the promise, believes God when He gives the promise, stretches out its hand when God offers[9] something, and accepts what He offers. This is the characteristic function of faith alone.[10]

6. Luther, *Luther's Works*, 7:275.

7. "The doctrine of the Gospel has been in the world ever since our first parents fell, and by various signs God confirmed the promise to the fathers. The earlier times knew nothing of the rainbow, circumcision, and other things that were ordained later on. But all ages had the knowledge of the Blessed Seed" (Luther, *Luther's Works*, 2:163–164).

8. Luther, *Luther's Works*, 3:156.

9. "The faith that justifies, however, is no mere historical knowledge, but the firm acceptance of God's offer promising forgiveness of sins and justification" (Tappert, *Book of Concord*, 114:48).

10. Luther, *Luther's Works*, 3:24.

This gospel is, strictly speaking, the promise of forgiveness of sins and justification[11] because of Christ.[12] It is the good news that

> we receive forgiveness of sins and become righteous before God by grace, for Christ's sake, through faith, when we believe that Christ suffered for us and that for His sake our sin is forgiven and righteousness and eternal life are given to us. For God will regard and reckon this faith as righteousness, as Paul says in Romans 3:21–26 and 4:5.[13]

As the Lutheran Church's *Book of Concord* says, "the law works wrath; it only accuses; it only terrifies consciences. Consciences cannot find peace unless they hear the voice of God, clearly promising the forgiveness of sins. Therefore it is necessary to add the Gospel promise, that for Christ's sake sins are forgiven and by faith in Christ we obtain the forgiveness of sins."[14]

> If you acknowledge and confess your iniquity and transgressions,[15] then My Son will be the propitiation[16]

11. "Therefore when a man believes that his sins are forgiven because of Christ and that God is reconciled and favorably disposed to him because of Christ, this personal faith obtains the forgiveness of sins and justifies us" (Tappert, *Book of Concord*, 113:45). "Faith alone justifies because we receive the forgiveness of sins and the Holy Spirit by faith alone" (Tappert, *Book of Concord*, 119:86). The word "justify" is used in a judicial way to mean "to absolve a guilty man and pronounce him righteous, and to do so on account of someone else's righteousness, namely, Christ's" (Tappert, *Book of Concord*, 154:305).

12. Tappert, *Book of Concord*, 113:43.

13. Tappert, *Book of Concord*, 30:1–3.

14. Tappert, *Book of Concord*, 144:257.

15. "This knowledge of our sin is the beginning of our salvation, that we completely despair of ourselves and give to God alone the glory for our righteousness" (Luther, *Luther's Works*, 2:41).

16. "Since Christ is set forth to be the propitiator, through whom the Father is reconciled to us, we cannot appease God's wrath by setting forth our own works. For it is only by faith that Christ is accepted as the mediator" (Tappert, *Book of Concord*, 118:80). Christ "was given for us to make satisfaction for the sins of the world and has been appointed as the mediator and the propitiator" (Tappet, *Book of Concord*, 112:40).

> for your sins; He will be your sanctification, redemption, righteousness and wisdom.[17]

Since this faith is a new life, it necessarily produces new impulses[18] and new works. For when faith takes hold of Christ, the mediator, the heart is at peace and begins to love God and to keep the law.[19]

17. Luther, *Luther's Works*, 7:281.

18. We are reborn not only for life but also for righteousness and "that newness of life through which we are zealous to obey God as we are taught by the Word and aided by the Holy Spirit. But this righteousness has merely its beginning in this life, and it cannot attain perfection in this flesh. Nevertheless, it pleases God, not as though it were a perfect righteousness or a payment for sin but because it comes from the heart and depends on its trust in the mercy of God through Christ" (Luther, *Luther's Works*, 1:64). "Since faith brings the Holy Spirit and produces a new life in our hearts, it must also produce spiritual impulses in our hearts" (Tappert, *Book of Concord*, 124:125). "After we have been justified and regenerated by faith, therefore, we begin to fear and love God, to pray and to expect help from Him, to thank and praise Him, and to submit to Him in our afflictions. Then we also begin to love our neighbor because our hearts have spiritual and holy impulses" (Tappert, *Book of Concord*, 124:125).

19. "We teach that a man is justified when, with his conscience terrified by the preaching of penitence, he takes heart and believes that he has a gracious God for Christ's sake. This faith is accounted for righteousness before God (Romans 4:3, 5). When the heart is encouraged and quickened by faith in this way, it receives the Holy Spirit. Through his renewal we can keep the law, love God and His Word, obey God in the midst of afflictions, and practice chastity, love toward our neighbor, and so forth. Even though they are a long way from the perfection of the law, these works please God on account of the justifying faith that for Christ's sake we have a gracious God" (Tappert, *Book of Concord*, 152:292–93).

The Will of His Good Pleasure[20]

His Incarnation Reveals the Father's Heart

After Adam and Eve had sinned, the Father revealed his heart and pointed to a deliverance through the seed[21] of a woman. The Father could have brought his Son into the world without a mother, but he wanted to make use of the female sex. He could likewise have formed a body suddenly from a virgin, just as he formed Adam from clay and Eve from a rib of Adam, but he did not choose to do this; he adhered to the order that he himself had established.

> Through the woman you, Satan, set upon and seduced the man, so that through sin you might be their head and master. But I, in turn, shall lie in wait for you by means of the same instrument. I shall snatch away the woman, and from her I shall produce a Seed, and that Seed will crush your head.[22]

Thus this promise and this threat are very clear and yet they are also very indefinite, for they leave the devil in such a state that

20. "This will of the divine good pleasure was ordained from eternity and was revealed and displayed in Christ" (Luther, *Luther's Works*, 2:48); for "it is impossible for the heart to take courage unless it considers this will of good pleasure, that is, the Son of God, who portrays for us the heart and will of the Father; namely, that He does not want to be angry with sinners but wants to show them mercy through His Son" (Luther, *Luther's Works*, 2:49). "Thus God reveals His will to us through Christ and the Gospel" (Luther, *Luther's Works*, 5:49).

21. "Because all these benefits are promised through this Seed, it is very clear that after the Fall our human nature could not, by its own strength, remove sin, escape the punishments of sin and death or recover the lost obedience" (Luther, *Luther's Works*, 1:196). "And so the Son of God had to become a sacrifice to achieve these things for us, to take away sin, to swallow up death, and to restore the lost obedience" (Luther, *Luther's Works*, 1:197).

22. Luther, *Luther's Works*, 1:193. "You [Satan] have corrupted the flesh through sin and have made it subject to death, but from that very flesh I shall bring forth a Man who will crush and prostrate you and all your powers" (Luther, *Luther's Works*, 1:193).

he suspects all mothers[23] of giving birth to this seed, although only one woman was to be the mother of the Blessed Seed.[24]

By calling his wife Eve, Adam gave evidence that he believed and understood the saying concerning the woman's seed who would crush the head of the serpent. Adam also used his wife's name[25] "as a means of finding comfort in the life which was to be restored through the promised Seed, who would crush the serpent's head and would slay the slayer himself."[26]

Therefore, as people reflect on Christ's incarnation, they are able to look into the very heart of God. As one gazes upon the Child lying in Mary's lap or upon the sacrificial victim suspended on the cross, we are able to view the very heart and will of the Father. There we shall see that he is compassionate and does not desire the death of the sinner, but that the sinner should turn from his way and live.

His Coming Reveals the Hidden God[27]

> From an unrevealed God I will become a revealed God. Nevertheless, I will remain the same God. I will be made flesh or I will send My Son . . . look at Him as He lies in the manger and on the lap of His mother, as He hangs on

23. "Thus because God is threatening in general when He says her Seed, He is mocking Satan and making him afraid of all women" (Luther, *Luther's Works*, 1:193).

24. Luther, *Luther's Works*, 1:193.

25. "By assigning this name to his wife he gives clear indication that the Holy Spirit had cheered his heart through his trust in the forgiveness of sins by the Seed of Eve" (Luther, *Luther's Works*, 1:220).

26. Luther, *Luther's Works*, 1:221.

27. "If you believe in the revealed God and accept His Word, He will gradually also reveal the hidden God; for he who sees Me also sees the Father as John 14:9 says. He who rejects the Son also loses the unrevealed God along with the revealed God" (Luther, *Luther's Works*, 5:46). "Therefore the godly should be aware and be intent only on learning to cling to the Child and Son Jesus, who is your God and was made flesh for your sake . . . if you have Him, then you also have the hidden God together with Him who has been revealed. And that is the only way, the truth and the life" (Luther, *Luther's Works*, 5:48).

> the cross. Observe what He does and what He says. There you will surely take hold of Me.[28]

In *Bondage of the Will* Luther makes the distinction between the hidden and the revealed God. God, in his majesty, is hidden and inaccessible to man. We cannot find or see him as he is. Yet, in his grace and out of his great love for us, he has chosen to take the form of the Word become flesh, born in Bethlehem.

In his incarnation, God himself would be present yet hidden and concealed. In Christ, God is found, and outside of the person born of Mary he is not to be found. Therefore, he who encounters this flesh encounters God. It is the purpose of his concealment that he can be seen, touched, and apprehended without the beholder being consumed by his majesty. If one is to meet God, he must come to Christ. His incarnation[29] is the only view of the Divinity[30] permitted and possible in this life.

Yet his presence can be seen and apprehended only by faith. It is only by faith, acquired through the word, that a person can cut through the coverings of flesh and blood and see him in Christ's incarnation.

Jacob's Ladder: The Mystery of His Incarnation

It is the dream of Jacob, when he sees a ladder set upon the earth with its top reaching into heaven and angels descending and ascending, that reveals the mystery of the incarnation in which the same person is both true God and true man. As the angels

28. Luther, *Luther's Works*, 5:45.

29. "For God's incarnation was foretold in order that we might have a definite pattern for recognizing and taking hold of God" (Luther, *Luther's Works*, 4:133).

30. "The incarnate Son of God is, therefore, the covering in which the Divine Majesty presents Himself to us with all His gifts, and does so in such a manner that there is no sinner too wretched to be able to approach Him with the firm assurance of obtaining pardon. This is the one and only view of the Divinity that is available and possible in this life" (Luther, *Luther's Works*, 2:49).

descend[31] they adore the child at his mother's breast and the man on the cross. As they ascend, they behold the Son of God from all eternity. If they look down, they see God subject to demons and to every creature. If they lift up their eyes, they see the incomprehensible majesty of God above them. Thus the ladder is the wonderful union of his divinity with our flesh.

His flesh must be true flesh "born from a flesh outstandingly sinful and contaminated by . . . sin."[32] As one of many examples, Luther recalls the story of Tamar becoming pregnant by Judah through the shameful act of incest.[33] Moreover, if he is to be the Savior of the world and not just of the Jewish people, gentile seed must be mixed with that of Abraham so that he would be born of and for all people. Therefore his father's side was Israelite but his mother's side there were gentiles, Moabites, Assyrians, Egyptians, and Canaanites.[34]

31. The angels constantly look at his divinity and humanity. "And now they descend from heaven after He has been made man. Now they look upon Christ and wonder at the work of the incarnation. They see that He has been made man, humiliated, and placed on His mother's lap. They adore the man who was crucified and rejected, and they acknowledge Him as the Son of God" (Luther, *Luther's Works*, 5:221).

32. Judah "committed this unspeakable act of incest in order that Christ might be born from a flesh outstandingly sinful and contaminated by a most disgraceful sin. For he begets twins by an incestuous harlot, his own daughter-in-law, and from this source the line of the Savior is later derived" (Luther, *Luther's Works*, 7:12).

33. There Tamar "was made pregnant by the most shameful act of incest, and the flesh from which Christ was to be born was poured from the loins of Judah and was propagated, carried about, and contaminated with sin right up to the conception of Christ. This is how our Lord God treats our Savior. God allows Him to be conceived in most disgraceful incest, in order that He may assume the truest flesh, just as our flesh is poured forth, conceived, and nourished in sins" (Luther, *Luther's Works*, 7:31).

34. "Special mention is made of Tamar, Ruth, Rahab, and Bathsheba. By this avenue the Gentiles come into communion and fellowship with the people of Israel, not only in the matter of religion but also in the matter of the same flesh . . . therefore Jews and Gentiles are now one flesh and born from one flesh" (Luther, *Luther's Works*, 7:14). "For on their father's side they are Israelites; but on their mother's side they are Gentiles, Moabites, Assyrians, Egyptians, and Canaanites" (Luther, *Luther's Works*, 7:15). "Christ our Lord

At the same time, his flesh was purified and sanctified by the power of the Holy Spirit. "It is descended from the accursed, lost, and condemned seed and flesh; nevertheless, it is without sin and corruption." According to his human nature, "Christ has the same flesh that we have; but in his conception the Holy Spirit came and overshadowed and purified the mass which He received from the virgin that he might be united with the divine nature."[35]

Finally, this dream was given to Jacob that he might understand that his incarnation would take place in a definite place. "Because the land of Canaan is promised to the descendants of Abraham and Christ was to be born of the descendants of Abraham, it is certain that Christ will be born in the land of Canaan and from the Jews."[36] For throughout all ages there had to be one definite family[37] from which alone it would be believed that Christ was to be born, so that the whole world might be assured that he who was born in this land in accordance with the promise is the true Savior and Blesser.

This very place would become the place of his earthly ministry[38] as he preached, healed, and taught. Luther even went so far

---

wanted to be born from the blood of various nations; for He had Rahab, Ruth and Tamar as mothers" (Luther, *Luther's Works*, 7:201).

35. Luther, *Luther's Works*, 7:36.

36. Luther, *Luther's Works*, 2:237.

37. "Therefore He revealed to Jacob himself [in Jacob's dream] that he would be the father of Christ and that the Son of Man would be born from his seed" (Luther, *Luther's Works*, 5:217).

38. "Thus the center of Paradise was where Jerusalem, Bethlehem, and Jericho were located later on, the places where Christ and John spent the greater part of their life" (Luther, *Luther's Works*, 1:310). This region, surmised Luther, was the very place where Adam, Abel, and Noah brought sacrifices and where the patriarch Shem made his dwelling (Luther, *Luther's Works*, 4:100). Thus, before the flood, "paradise was near that land, and . . . Adam dwelt in the neighborhood of Mt. Moriah after he had been driven from Paradise. Consequently, even before the Flood it was a famous place because of the worship of God, and it remained famous up to the time of Christ" (Luther, *Luther's Works*, 4:100–101). "But after the Holy Spirit was bestowed [at Pentecost], the Gospel was spread from there into the entire world; and no longer was either the worship of God or the church confined to that small corner of the Jewish land" (Luther, *Luther's Works*, 4:101).

as to maintain that he was crucified[39] at this very place, slept in the sepulcher, and rose where the angels ascended and descended.

In summary, this Blessed Seed would be a human being whom people could see, touch, hear, and feel. This Jesus is indeed the "right man"[40] who was set plainly before our eyes. At the same time, he must be true God because only the Son of God is able to reveal God. Moreover, this Blessed Seed[41] will bring a blessing so long and wide that it will reach all of the families of the earth. If the seed of Abraham does this, he must be a human being by nature; on the other hand, if he blesses others, he "must be true God, because to deliver all nations from the curse is the work of God." Therefore, this seed must be "true God and [true] man in one person."[42]

39. "It is possible that later on Calvary, where Christ offered Himself for the sins of the world, was located where the tree of the knowledge of good and evil had been while Paradise was still standing" (Luther, *Luther's Works*, 1:310). "Therefore it was God's will that Christ should be crucified and die here, and that the place where Jacob saw the ladder should be the same place where Christ, the true Jacob, slept in the sepulcher and rose again and the angels descended and ascended" (Luther, *Luther's Works*, 5:243).

40. Luther, *Luther's Works*, 53:285

41. The seed of Abraham "is the principal, effective cause of that blessing . . .[yet] He is not only the effective cause; but He is also the formal cause, that is, the blessing itself" (Luther, *Luther's Works*, 4:157).

42. "The blessing fits the Creator alone and not any creature. Hence He who blesses must be true God, because to deliver all nations from the curse is a work of God, not of man or of angels. And so the Seed is true God and man in one Person. He is man because He is of the Seed of Abraham; He is God because He bestows the blessing" (Luther, *Luther's Works*, 4:160). "This blessing is so powerful and efficacious that it is able to destroy and abolish both death and the entire curse which was brought on as a result of original sin" (Luther, *Luther's Works*, 4:161).

Jacob Wrestling with God: The Nature of Faith[43]

Later in Jacob's life, the Lord came to him and wrestled[44] with him until daybreak. This man, the Lord in disguise, exercises Jacob until the firmness of faith shows itself. Jacob, by his faith, was able to conquer God just as the Canaanite woman[45] was able to cling to Christ when Jesus opposed her (Matt 15:21–28).

> Her faith was very sharply attacked when He called her a dog. But she came back at Him, saying: "Seeing that you called me a dog, give me the crumbs which fall from the tables of the masters and which belong to the dogs." This was assuredly a beautiful and illustrious faith and an outstanding example which shows the method and skill of striving with God. For we should not immediately cast aside courage and all hope at the first blow but press on, pray, seek and knock.[46]

After the wrestling had ended, Christ laid aside his mask and spoke life-giving words to Jacob (Gen 32:22–30). He revealed himself as the one who rewards those who persistently seek him and cling to him in faith; for he is the man who exercises[47] Jacob

43. "It is the nature of faith to believe with certainty that we are blessed, not through ourselves but through Christ, who is our blessing" (Luther, *Luther's Works*, 4:171).

44. "But our opinion is this, that the wrestler is the Lord of glory, God Himself, or God's Son, who was to become incarnate and who appeared and spoke to the fathers" (Luther, *Luther's Works*, 6:130). "The man wrestling with Jacob was our Lord Jesus Christ Himself, the Son of God" (Luther, *Luther's Works*, 6:185). "I have seen the Lord face to face. And now I see clearly, Jacob says, that the wrestler who tested me was God Himself" (Luther, *Luther's Works*, 6:144).

45. "So it makes its appearance in the Canaanite woman, with whom Jesus was wrestling when He said: You are a dog, the bread of the sons does not belong to you (Matthew 15:26). The woman did not yield here but offered opposition, saying: Even the dogs eat the crumbs that fall from their master's tables. And so she was victorious and heard the excellent word of praise: O woman, great is your faith!" (Luther, *Luther's Works*, 6:139).

46. Luther, *Luther's Works*, 6:140.

47. "The exercises of faith are necessary for the godly; for without them their faith would grow weak and lukewarm, yes, would eventually be

until his faith shows itself. As evidence of his faith, Jacob's name is changed by God himself. In this test, and in the changing of Jacob's name, Jesus sought not to destroy Jacob but to confirm and strengthen him in the promise.

He also came in this way so that Jacob, and his descendants, would know that one day he would dwell among them in human flesh and that only by faith can anyone accept the revelation that he is true God and true man. It is God's way to play with us until faith shows itself; but, after the wrestling had ended, he laid down his mask and rewarded Jacob, who clung to him by faith.

The Will of the Sign[48]

Old Testament Signs

God is not a vagabond, naked God but rather one who has clothed himself with definite signs in a specific place. These definite signs are divine coverings[49] through which he reveals[50] himself and his will to us. Wherever the visible sign is, there God is truly present[51]

extinguished" (Luther, *Luther's Works*, 5:56). It is the history of the saints that "they hear the Word, believe it, and are exercised in faith by many tribulations and annoyances" (Luther, *Luther's Works*, 5:266).

48. "Now the operation of God is called the will of the sign; for He comes out toward us to deal with us through some sort of covering and external object we can grasp, such as the Word of God and the ceremonies He has instituted" (Luther, *Luther's Works*, 2:47). Thus, through the will of the sign "God deals with us within the range of our comprehension. Therefore these alone must engage our attention" (Luther, *Luther's Works*, 2:47). "For God does not want to rule us in accordance with His secret will; He wants to do so in accordance with His will as it has been ordered and revealed by His Word" (Luther, *Luther's Works*, 3:289).

49. "Thus we have the promises of Baptism, of the Lord's Supper, of the Keys, etc., in which God sets before us His will, His mercy, and His works" (Luther, *Luther's Works*, 1:304).

50. "But the God who has revealed Himself by visible marks, who has given the Word of promise and has instituted the sacraments, is the true God and Savior whom we are able to take hold of and to understand" (Luther, *Luther's Works*, 3:122).

51. "I have always displayed Myself to the eyes and ears of men in such a

wrapped up in the garment of the sign. Through them God deals with us within the range of our comprehension, being both covered and revealed.

After the fall of Adam and Eve into sin, God, in his mercy, enveloped himself in a gentle breeze. He did this, first of all, so that he could reveal himself to Adam under a cover and, secondly, that in his coming in a very soft breeze he would bring a fatherly reprimand. Later, in the sacrifices,[52] we see God's will that some outward and visible sign of his grace be placed alongside the word so that human beings might be reminded of his mercy and would believe with greater assurance that he is kind and merciful. In this sign[53] Adam could perceive that he had not been cast off by God but that he was still the object of God's concern and regard.

Later, circumcision was given to Abraham and his descendants as a sign and sacrament[54] through which they would be made righteous if they would embrace and believe the promise

---

way that they could become aware of My presence in the sacrifices, in circumcision, in burning incense, in the cloud, in the Red Sea, in the manna, in the brazen serpent, in the tabernacle of Moses, in the temple of Solomon, and in the cloud. And it was My delight to display and reveal Myself in this manner to the children of men" (Luther, *Luther's Works*, 1:248).

52. "God revealed His grace in the sacrifices and gave His approval of them by kindling and consuming them with fire" (Luther, *Luther's Works*, 1:250). "Thus prior to circumcision the sacrifices were signs. The brothers Abel and Cain bring sacrifices. For Abel the sacrifice is a seal of righteousness, because he believes. For Cain, however, it is not a seal of righteousness, because he does not believe but retains the bare work without faith" (Luther, *Luther's Works*, 3:106). "Abel's offerings were pleasing and acceptable because he offered them in fear and faith, and strove by means of this gift to manifest a grateful heart. When the heart is offered, this is by far the most pleasing gift to God" (Luther, *Luther's Works*, 7:322).

53. "Men were to have signs by means of which they might comfort themselves in their sins and gain courage through their reliance on divine grace. It is not the worth of the work itself that is of value in the sacrifice; it is the mercy and power of the divine promise, because God prescribes this form of worship and promises that it will be pleasing to Him" (Luther, *Luther's Works*, 1:250).

54. "But circumcision not only brought this people together politically and served as a password among them; but it was also a sacrament, that is, a sign of the divine will and therefore a sign of eternal salvation for those who believed" (Luther, *Luther's Works*, 3:110).

connected with it.[55] But circumcision was more; it was a sign to the nations that the promised Savior[56] would be born[57] from this circumcised nation. In this way, God has always provided some public sign[58] whereby the nations[59] might find the true God.

> For we have need of marks and signs of this kind, in order that they may lead us to the knowledge of God, since

55. "Thus circumcision was enjoined upon Abraham in order that for his descendants it might be a sacrament through which they would be made righteous if they believed the promise which the Lord attached to it" (Luther, *Luther's Works*, 3:87).

56. "For this law concerning circumcision was imposed on the Jews, not in order that they might be justified by it—for then Christ would have been promised in vain—but in order that they might be a people separated from all other peoples, in order that it might be known from what people, from what part of the world, the Savior was to be born" (Luther, *Luther's Works*, 3:82). Circumcision was entrusted to Abraham as to a standard bearer "in order that through circumcision all nations might have a definite place and a definite person in whom God would appear visibly and in association with whom they would find the true God, who was to be found nowhere else in the world" (Luther, *Luther's Works*, 3:126).

57. For what benefit was circumcision given? "To make known that the Savior was to be born from this circumcised nation and not from the Gentiles. He who was desired by all the nations did not become incarnate among all the nations; He became incarnate among this one people which had been commanded by God to be circumcised" (Luther, *Luther's Works*, 3:91). "Thus circumcision, too, was a visible form which was not instituted by human beings but was instituted by God Himself, in order that He might be known through it and that not only the Jews but also the heathen might believe in that God who had revealed Himself to the Jews in such a manner" (Luther, *Luther's Works*, 3:109–10).

58. "From the beginning of the world divine wisdom has so ordained and arranged things that there was always some public sign toward which all people might look, in order that the Gentiles, too, might find, worship, and pray to the true God, although not all who had that sign believed and had use of it for righteousness" (Luther, *Luther's Works*, 3:106). Thus, "God establishes a sign of grace, in order that it may be recognized by sinners and sinners may be saved" (Luther, *Luther's Works*, 3:107).

59. "For God is the God of the Jews and of the Gentiles; and although there is a difference in this respect, that the Jews have the promise and their own distinctive marks by which they are known to be the people of God, nevertheless God does not exclude the Gentiles from the promise, provided that they embrace it in faith" (Luther, *Luther's Works*, 3:96).

> human reason is unable to find God unless such signs instituted by God lead us by the hand, so to speak. And nothing is more dangerous than if one devises his own way to God and relies on his own speculations.[60]

Therefore circumcision, like the sacrifices, was raised up as a sign to be looked at and be recognized by those sinners who were to be saved. Circumcision was more than just a unifying rite instituted for political unity and solidarity. It was a sign of the divine will and therefore a sign of eternal salvation for those who believed.

In our human weakness and comprehension we are in need of such signs so that we might find him but also so that we do not seek him in some other way. Thus, prior to circumcision, the ministry of the word and the sacrifices were visible signs of the invisible grace; but circumcision, which was instituted under Abraham, had validity up to the coming of the Blessed Seed.

New Testament Signs[61]

Since the coming of Christ, God continues to speak to us in a fatherly manner through the ministry of the word, his sacraments, and his promises of eternal grace. "Actually our glory in the New Testament is greater. We not only have God drawing near to us; we also have Him dwelling in us bodily."[62]

It is a great gift of his mercy that he is found, not in some faraway place, but in baptism, in the Lord's Supper, in the words of the gospel, in the use of the keys,[63] and with any brother or sister who

60. Luther, *Luther's Works*, 3:107.

61. "In the New Testament we have as a visible form the Son of God on the lap of His mother. He suffered and died for us, as the Creed teaches. Besides, we have other visible forms: Baptism, the Eucharist, and the spoken Word itself. Therefore we cannot complain of having been forsaken" (Luther, *Luther's Works*, 3:109).

62. Luther, *Luther's Works*, 3:169.

63. "I absolve you from your sins in the name of the Father and of the Son and of the Holy Spirit; that is, I reconcile your soul to God, remove from you God's wrath and displeasure, put you in His grace, and give you the inheritance

with me confesses and believes in the Son of God. These are the epiphanies[64] or appearances that are common for all Christians.

To us in the New Testament era, baptism and the Eucharist are our visible signs[65] of grace.[66] Just as the previous generation had circumcision[67] added as a distinguishing sign, so the new generation of Christ has other distinguishing signs such as baptism, which promises eternal life to those who believe.

These signs, along with the word, are our light bearers today, and wherever these are, there we find Christ,[68] the forgiveness of sins, and eternal life. As his people worship, Christ is present in and with his gifts of grace. As his word is preached and the sacraments are administered, Christ imparts the word through the medium of human tongues[69] and voices.

---

of eternal life and the kingdom of heaven" (Luther, *Luther's Works*, 5:140).

64. "But our God is He whom the Holy Scriptures show, because He gives us His epiphany, His appearance and speaks with us" (Luther, *Luther's Works*, 4:145).

65. "It is taught among us that the sacraments were instituted not only to be signs by which people might be identified outwardly as Christians, but that they are signs and testimonies of God's will toward us for the purpose of awakening and strengthening our faith" (Augsburg Confession, art. 13, quoted in Tappert, *Book of Concord*, 35:1).

66. "The sacraments are not only signs among men, but signs of God's will toward us . . . as signs of grace. There are two parts to a sacrament, the sign and the Word" (Apology of the Augsburg Confession, art. 24, quoted in Tappert, *Book of Concord*, 262:69).

67. "Abraham had circumcision as the sign of this promise. We have Baptism, which was instituted with a far more magnificent form; for we are baptized in the name of the Father, of the Son, and of the Holy Spirit" (Luther, *Luther's Works*, 3:123–24).

68. "To us in the New Testament, Baptism and the Eucharist have been given as visible signs of grace, so that we might firmly believe that our sins have been forgiven through Christ's suffering and that we have been redeemed by His death. Thus the church has never been deprived to such an extent of outward signs that it became impossible to know where God could be surely found" (Luther, *Luther's Works*, 1:248).

69. "Thus God is present in Baptism, in the Lord's Supper, and in the use of the Keys because His own Word is present there. Therefore even though we do not see or hear Him but see and hear the minister, God Himself is nevertheless truly present, baptizes and absolves. And in the Lord's Supper He is present in

> You have Baptism. You have the Sacrament of the Eucharist, where the bread and wine are the species, figures, and forms in which and under which God in person speaks and works into your ears, eyes and heart. Besides, you have the ministry of the Word and teachers through whom God speaks with you. You have the ministry of the Keys, through which He absolves and comforts you.[70]

In the pulpit he speaks through the mouth of the preacher, at the font he himself is the Baptizer, at the altar he imparts the remission of sins through the hands of the minister. It is God alone who operates, but he operates through us.

> It is true that you hear a human being when you are baptized and when you partake of the Holy Supper. But the Word with which you hear is not that of a human being; it is the Word of the living God. It is He who baptizes you; it is He who absolves you from sins; and it is He who commands you to hope in His mercy. It is great ingratitude to slight these faces[71] of God, as Scripture calls them, and meanwhile to look for other appearances and revelations.[72]

---

such an extraordinary way that the Son of God Himself gives us His body with the bread and His blood with the wine" (Luther, *Luther's Works*, 3:220).

70. Luther, *Luther's Works*, 5:21. "Through the Word and the rite God simultaneously moves the heart to believe and take hold of faith, as Paul says in Romans 10:17. . . . As the Word enters through the ears to strike the heart, so the rite itself enters through the eyes to move the heart. The Word and the rite have the same effect . . . for the rite is received by the eyes and is a sort of picture of the Word, signifying the same thing as the Word. Therefore both have the same effect" (AP XIII; Tappert, *Book of Concord*, 211–212:5).

71. "When I approach Baptism, I must certainly conclude that nothing human is being done here. But the water is a veil or a means. So is the Word with which God is veiled. Behind these stands our Lord God, and they are the faces of God through which He speaks with us and works in every person individually. He baptizes me; He absolves me and gives me His body and blood through the tongue and hand of the minister . . . and this is the presence or form or epiphany of God in these means" (Luther, *Luther's Works*, 8:145).

72. Luther, *Luther's Works*, 3:166.

Where these signs of grace are not present or where they are despised, there is not only no grace but all sorts of errors[73] and false forms of worship[74] and other signs. Those who want to be saved must hold "to the form, the signs, and the coverings of the Godhead, such as His Word and His works. For in His Word and in His works He shows Himself to us."[75] Therefore,

> Let it be the concern of each of us to abide by the signs by which God has revealed Himself to us, namely, His Son, born of the Virgin Mary and lying in His manger among the cattle; the Word; Baptism; the Lord's Supper; and absolution. In these images we see and meet a God whom we can bear, one who comforts us, lifts us up into hope, and saves us.[76]

73. "When the light of the Word and these signs of grace which have been given by God have been lost, men run, of necessity, after the desire of their hearts" (Luther, *Luther's Works*, 1:249).

74. "Thus Satan strives hard to lead us away from the forms prescribed by God. But you must adhere to and follow this sure and infallible rule: God in His divine wisdom arranges to manifest Himself to human beings by some definite and visible form which can be seen with the eyes and touched with the hands, in short, is within the scope of the five senses. So near to us does the Divine Majesty place Itself" (Luther, *Luther's Works*, 3:109). Therefore, "we are not permitted to institute or do anything, especially before God and in the worship of God, unless the Word instructs and commands us" (Luther, *Luther's Works*, 2:112).

75. Luther, *Luther's Works*, 1:13.

76. Luther, *Luther's Works*, 2:48.

Chapter 3

The True and False Church

The Kingdom of God and the Kingdom of the World

God and Satan, since the garden of Eden, are engaged in a great conflict for the soul of every single individual. God wants every person to be saved and Satan wants every person to perish eternally. Moreover, the world and its god (Satan) cannot and will not bear the word of the true God to be made known and the true God cannot and will not keep silent.

In the one kingdom, Satan reigns and holds captive to his will all those who have not been wrested from him by the Spirit of Christ; nor does the devil allow them to be plucked away by any other power but the Spirit of God, as Christ tells us in the parable of the strong man keeping his palace in peace (Matt 12:22–29).

In the other kingdom, Christ reigns. His kingdom continually resists and wars against that of Satan, and we are translated into his kingdom, not by our own power, but by the grace of God, which delivers us from this present evil age and from the dominion of darkness.[1]

As a result of this conflict, two kinds of people are derived from the two sons born to Adam. The whole course of history is the intermingling of two peoples, going back as far as Abel and Cain. Cain appears to be saintly but he is wicked and does not

1. Luther, *Luther's Works*, 33:287.

believe the promise concerning the Blessed Seed. Abel, on the other hand, does not rely on his worthiness or his work but on the plain promise that had been given concerning the woman's seed.

The Origin of the Two Churches

With Adam, Eve, and their descendants, we see that two generations of human beings are being dealt with: the one of the righteous, which is the true church; the other of the unrighteous, which is the false church. Thus, from the beginning, there is a twofold church in the world just as the seed is twofold.

Moreover, from the very beginning, the Creator ordained that humankind be busy with his word and with the forms of worship established by him. On the Sabbath day Adam would have admonished his descendants to live a holy and sinless life, to work faithfully in the garden, and to beware with the greatest care of the tree of the knowledge of good and evil.

It was also God's design that the tree of the knowledge of good and evil[2] be Adam's altar[3] and pulpit and the designated place where Adam, and his household, would come to worship God. There they would gather in order to hear the word of God and to bear witness through their obedience that they knew, honored, and feared God.

> Here he [Adam] was to yield to God the obedience he owed, give recognition to the Word and will of God, give thanks to God, and call upon God for aid against temptation.[4]

2. God "demands from Adam that at this tree of the knowledge of good and evil he demonstrate his reverence and obedience toward God and that he maintain this practice, as it were, of worshiping God by not eating anything from it" (Luther, *Luther's Works*, 1:94).

3. An altar "denotes that a certain place was appointed for teaching and hearing the Word of God" (Luther, *Luther's Works*, 4:89).

4. Luther, *Luther's Works*, 1:95.

Thus, God's command regarding the tree was to be an outward form of worship[5] and an outward work of obedience toward God. This tree was not deadly by nature but became so only by the word of God and Adam's and Eve's disobedience.

> It was God's intention that this command should provide man with an opportunity for obedience and outward worship, and that this tree should be a sort of sign by which man would give evidence that he was obeying God.[6]

However, as soon as God had given his word concerning the tree of the knowledge of good and evil, Satan made it his business to visit Eve with his own word so that Eve was tempted to doubt God's goodness[7] and to listen to another teacher. When God came to them and asked "Where are you?" God spoke words of law to their conscience. God wanted to show Adam and Eve that though they were hidden, they were not hidden from God, and when they avoided God, they did not escape God.[8]

After their consciences had been convicted[9] by the law, Adam and Eve were terrified and hid. This fear of Adam and Eve toward God was a clear indication that they had fallen completely from the faith.[10] Adam should have said, "Lord, I have sinned!" Instead,

5. "The tree is put before Adam in order that he may also have some outward, physical way of indicating his worship of God and of demonstrating his obedience by an outward work" (Luther, *Luther's Works*, 1:94).

6. Luther, *Luther's Works*, 1:154.

7. "This was the greatest and severest of all temptations; for the serpent directs its attack at God's good will and makes it its business to prove from the prohibition of the tree that God's will toward man is not good" (Luther, *Luther's Works*, 1:146). "Satan is seeking to deprive them [Adam and Eve] of the Word and the knowledge of God that they may reach the conclusion: this is not the will of God; God does not command this." (Luther, *Luther's Works*, 1:152).

8. Luther, *Luther's Works*, 1:173.

9. "Therefore it was not the nakedness that perplexed you, it was not My voice that frightened you; but your conscience convicted you of sin because you ate the fruit from the forbidden tree" (Luther, *Luther's Works*, 1:176).

10. Luther, *Luther's Works*, 1:170. "Their very action shows that their will has become depraved, because they have a desire for what is forbidden by God;

he accuses God of sin and transfers his guilt from himself to the Creator. Therefore, advises Luther,

> Do not flee from God when He is pointing His spear at you, but flee to Him with a humble confession of your guilt and a request for forgiveness. Then God will draw back His spear and spare you.[11]

Instead Adam tries to flee from God and his presence, and he answers God most stupidly, observed Luther.

> He wants to inform God that he is naked—God, who created him naked. . . . He says that he heard God's voice and was afraid. But had he not heard the voice of the Lord before, when He forbade him to eat of the forbidden tree? Why was he not afraid then? Why did he not hide then? Why did he stand glad and upright when he saw and heard God before him? But now he is terrified by the rustling of a leaf.[12]

In loving response to the sinful disobedience of Adam and Eve, God, in his grace and goodness, enveloped himself in a gentle breeze[13] so that he might reveal himself to Adam under a cover. It was a great comfort to them that, after they had lost paradise and the tree of life, God gave them another sign of grace, namely, the sacrifices. In this sign they could know that they had not been cast off by God but that they were still the object of his concern.

It was at that time that human beings began to call upon the name of the Lord.[14] From Adam the promise concerning Christ

---

they aspire to become disobedient to God but obedient to the devil" (Luther, *Luther's Works*, 1:172).

11. Luther, *Luther's Works*, 1:277.

12. Luther, *Luther's Works*, 1:174.

13. Luther, *Luther's Works*, 1:11. "But God comes in a very soft breeze to indicate that the reprimand will be fatherly. He does not drive Adam away from Himself because of his sin, but He calls him and calls him back from his sin" (Luther, *Luther's Works*, 1:180–81).

14. "At that time men began to call upon the name of the Lord, that is, that Adam, Seth, and Enos exhorted their descendants to wait for their redemption, to believe the promise about the woman's Seed and through that hope to

is passed on to Seth and others who exhorted their descendants to wait for their redemption and to believe that promise concerning the one who would deliver them through woman's seed. Therefore this

> doctrine of the Gospel has been in the world since our first parents fell, and by various signs God confirmed this promise to the fathers. The earlier times knew nothing of the rainbow, circumcision, and other things that were ordained later on. But all ages had the knowledge of the Blessed Seed.[15]

Alongside this gospel, the good news concerning the Blessed Seed, the sacrifices provided an outward and visible sign of his grace. For "Abel and Cain had been accustomed by their father to sacrifice, which at that time was the proper form for the worship of God."[16]

Moreover, it is with the sacrifices of Abel and Cain[17] that we begin to differentiate between the true and false church. Cain

---

overcome the treachery, the crosses, the persecutions, the hatreds, the wrongs, etc. of the Cainites; not to despair about their salvation but rather to thank God, who one day would deliver them through the woman's Seed" (Luther, *Luther's Works*, 1:328). "For the false church is always the persecutor of the true church, not only spiritually, by means of false doctrine and ungodly forms of worship; but physically, by means of the sword and tyranny" (Luther, *Luther's Works*, 2:214).

15. Luther, *Luther's Works*, 2:163–64.

16. "The church cannot exist without the constant use of the Word, and the church always had its sacraments, or tokens of grace, and its ceremonies. Thus Abel and Cain had been accustomed by their father to sacrifice, which at that time was the proper form for the worship of God; and they continued to offer sacrifices" (Luther, *Luther's Works*, 2:197).

17. "When two sons had been born to Adam, two kinds of people took their origin from them" (Luther, *Luther's Works*, 2:210). Later, with the offspring of Abraham, there were "Ishmael and Isaac, the natural sons of Abraham, [who] denote two peoples: Ishmael, the people of the flesh; Isaac, the people of the Spirit or of the promise" (Luther, *Luther's Works*, 3:192). Thus, there is a threefold progeny of Abraham: "The first is physical and without the promise concerning Christ. Ishmael, who was born of the flesh of Abraham, was an offspring of this kind. The second progeny is physical, but with the promise concerning Christ. Thus Isaac, too, was born of the flesh of Abraham;

appears to be saintly but he is ungodly and does not believe the divine promise concerning the Blessed Seed. Abel, on the other hand, "by faith[18] took hold of the promise given to Adam concerning the Seed; and this faith[19] is also the reason why he offered a better sacrifice than Cain."[20]

> If you look at the work itself, you cannot prefer Abel to Cain . . . the fault lay not in the materials which were offered[21] but in the person who brought the offering. The faith[22] of the individual was the weight which added value to Abel's offering, but Cain spoiled his offering. Abel believes that God is good and merciful. For this reason his sacrifice is pleasing to God.[23]

---

but he had the promise. . . . The third progeny is not physical but is of the offspring only of the promise" (Luther, *Luther's Works*, 4:25–26). Sadly, noted Luther, the Jews "have lost the true doctrine concerning the promise and faith; and they cling simply to the physical birth, which by itself alone is nothing unless the promise and faith are added" (Luther, *Luther's Works*, 4:27).

18. Hebrews 11:4.

19. "We teach and confess that a person rather than his work is accepted by God and that a person does not become righteous as a result of a righteous work; but that a work becomes righteous and good as a result of a righteous and good person" (Luther, *Luther's Works*, 1:257). "Abel, rather than his work, was righteous and . . . the work pleases because of the person, not the person because of the work" (Luther, *Luther's Works*, 1:257). "He [God] is interested in faith alone, that is, the reliance on His mercy through Christ. Through it people begin to please God, and after that their works also please Him" (Luther, *Luther's Works*, 1:259). Moreover, "nothing is pleasing to God unless it is done in faith" (Luther, *Luther's Works*, 1:265).

20. Cain "did not believe the promise concerning Christ. Abel, on the contrary, by faith took hold of the promise given to Adam concerning the Seed; and this faith is also the reason why he offered a better sacrifice than Cain" (Luther, *Luther's Works*, 1:246).

21. "God does not have regard for either the size or the quantity or even the value of the work, but simply for the faith of the individual. Similarly, by contrast, God does not despise the smallness, the lack of value, or the lowly nature of the work, but only a person's lack of faith" (Luther, *Luther's Works*, 1:258).

22. "God wants to teach us that we are saved by grace alone or by faith alone. Faith takes hold of the grace that is set before us in the promise" (Luther, *Luther's Works*, 4:60).

23. Luther, *Luther's Works*, 1:251.

Thus Cain's offering did not please because the unbelieving Cain did not please. On the other hand, Abel's offering pleased because Abel pleased; and this was so because of his faith, "since it did not rely on his own worthiness, his sacrifices, or his work, but on the plain promise which had been given about the woman's Seed."[24]

> Thus prior to circumcision the sacrifices were signs. The brothers Abel and Cain bring sacrifices. For Abel the sacrifice is a seal of righteousness, because he believes. For Cain, however, it is not a seal of righteousness, because he does not believe but retains the bare work without faith.[25]

Later on, when Abraham was nearly swallowed up by the false church of Nimrod and its Babylonian religion, God called him out of idolatry through the ministry of Shem and directed him to separate from the ungodly race and seek a new dwelling place. Abraham is "seize[d] through the Word and form[ed] into a new . . . being";[26] of himself, Abraham is nothing but an idolater, but through God's mercy, he is freed from sin, death,[27] and damnation through Christ the Blessed Seed.[28] Moreover, Abraham was not justified because he forsook everything when he went out from Ur of the Chaldeans. Rather,

> He had already been justified[29] when he believed the promise of God that was revealed through the holy

24. Luther, *Luther's Works*, 1:259.

25. Luther, *Luther's Works*, 3:106.

26. "For what is Abraham except a man who hears God when He calls him" (Luther, *Luther's Works*, 2:246). "Abraham is merely the material that the Divine Majesty seizes through the Word and forms into a new human being and into a patriarch" (Luther, *Luther's Works*, 2:247).

27. "Those who accept the teaching of the Gospel lose nothing except their sins and eternal death, but gain freedom from all idolatry and from the rule of Satan" (Luther, *Luther's Works*, 1:192).

28. Luther, *Luther's Works*, 2:247.

29. This righteousness of Abraham, which is his by faith alone, "is prior to the Law, prior to the works of the Law, prior to the people of the Law and before Moses, the lawgiver, was born" (Luther, *Luther's Works*, 3:20). Abraham

> patriarchs. . . . Therefore he heard the Word and believed the Word;[30] and later on, after he had been justified thereby, he also became a righteous doer of works by wandering about and following Christ, who had called him.[31]

The House of God and the Gate of Heaven

> Wherever the Word is heard, where Baptism, the Sacrament of the Altar, and absolution are administered, there you must determine and conclude with certainty: This is surely God's house; here heaven has been opened.[32]

Therefore "direct your step to the place where the Word resounds and the sacraments are administered, and there write the title the gate of God."[33] As we gather at these external places to hear a sermon delivered through a human voice, and gather at temples built of stones and wood to receive the sacraments, we must always remember that here is the house of God and the gate of heaven; for God Himself is speaking.

> I hear a man's voice. I see human gestures. The bread and the wine in the Supper are physical things. At ordination the hands of carnal men are imposed. In Baptism water is water. For the flesh judges in no other way concerning all these matters. But if you look at that addition with spiritual eyes, namely, at whose Word it is that is spoken

believed God and God reckoned it to him as righteousness. This passage "constructs the foremost article of our faith—the article that is intolerable to the world and to Satan—namely, that faith alone justifies, but that faith consists in giving assent to the promises of God and concluding that they are true" (Luther, *Luther's Works*, 3:19).

30. "Faith alone lays hold of the promise, believes God when He gives the promise, stretches out its hand when God offers something, and accepts what He offers" (Luther, *Luther's Works*, 3:24).

31. Luther, *Luther's Works*, 2:269–70.

32. Luther, *Luther's Works*, 5:244.

33. Luther, *Luther's Works*, 5:247.

> and heard there, not indeed the word of a man—for if it is the word of a man, then the devil is speaking—but the Word of God, then you will understand that it is the house of God and the gate of heaven.[34]

And yet, if the church is to be the house of God,[35] it is necessary for it to have the word of God and for God alone to be the head of the household in this house; for it is a house in which he speaks with us, deals with us, feeds us, and cares for us.

Wherever the Word Is Heard, There Is the Church

Wherever the word is heard, there is the church, for it is God's word[36] that establishes the church. Consequently, the church exists only where the word is and where there are people who believe the word; for there is no people of God unless it has the promises and believes them.[37] Thus, "where the Word is, there the church is, there the Spirit is, there Christ is."[38]

> But just as the Word is not bound to any place, so the Church is not bound to any place. . . . But where God speaks, where Jacob's ladder[39] is, where the angels ascend

34. Luther, *Luther's Works*, 5:248.

35. "The church is the house of God which leads from earth to heaven. The place of the church is in the temple, in the school, in the home, and in the bedchamber. Wherever two or three gather in the name of Christ, there God dwells" (Luther, *Luther's Works*, 5:250). "For where God dwells, there the church is, and nowhere else; for the church is God's house and the gate of heaven, where the entrance to eternal life and the departure from the earthly to the heavenly life are open" (Luther, *Luther's Works*, 5:245).

36. "The church is the daughter who is born from the Word; she is not the mother of the Word" (Luther, *Luther's Works*, 2:101).

37. "There can be neither faith nor worship of God where there is no Word, and wherever the Word is, there must be some who believe. Where, then, these two are, there follows the third, namely, the cross and mortification. These three make up the Christian life" (Luther, *Luther's Works*, 4:101).

38. "For these cannot be separated: where the Word is, there the church is, there the Spirit is, there Christ is" (Luther, *Luther's Works*, 2:229).

39. "For wherever Christ, the Blessed Seed rules, there the church is" (Luther, *Luther's Works*, 3:152).

> and descend, there the church is, there the Kingdom of heaven is opened.[40]

There is nothing more precious in the world than the church where his voice is heard and where God is worshiped with true forms of worship, that is, with faith, invocation, patience and obedience. Therefore the true church is made up of those who have the promise and believe it. The false church rejects these promises of God and concerns itself with things that he has not commanded nor promised.

This is the great difference between the godly and the ungodly: among the godly there is the word; on the other side there is silence.[41]

The Bed Is Too Narrow

Unregenerate man longs for a different wisdom, a wisdom apart from the word. When he is not satisfied with the knowledge contained in the word, he wants to rise higher and know God in a way different from his revelation of himself in his word.

The great danger for the church is our sleeping eyes and dull ears whereby we slight these faces of God.[42] This is what happened

40. Luther, *Luther's Works*, 5:244. Thus the church is established "that it may be the gate of heaven and that we may pass from this earthly life into the eternal and heavenly life" (Luther, *Luther's Works*, 5:250). "The church is the place or the people where God dwells for the purpose of bringing us into the kingdom of heaven, for it is the gate of heaven" (Luther, *Luther's Works*, 5:250). "This, then, is the complete definition of the church which is the habitation of God on earth. Not that we should remain on earth, but the sacraments are administered and the Word is taught in order that we may be led into the kingdom of heaven and through the church may enter into heaven" (Luther, *Luther's Works*, 5:250).

41. Luther, *Luther's Works*, 4:376.

42. "Perhaps God appeared to Adam without a covering, but after the Fall into sin He appeared in a gentle breeze as though enveloped in a covering. Similarly He was enveloped later on in the tabernacle by the mercy seat and in the desert by cloud and fire. Moses, therefore, calls these objects 'faces of God,' through which God manifested Himself" (Luther, *Luther's Works*, 1:11). It was the understanding of Luther that the face of God involved "those things

to the carnal descendants of Abraham who despised the visible signs of their generation and devised their own way. Yet, in the church, nothing should be heard or seen except what God does; for it is error to rely on one's thinking alone apart from, and without, the word of God.

Moreover, wherever the word is, there Satan[43] is active and seeks to spread false teaching[44] by corrupting the word of God in such a way[45] that human beings doubt the goodness[46] of God. Satan seeks to rob humankind of God as he fabricates[47] a new god who exists nowhere and to institute forms of worship[48] in which

by which God shows that He is with us" (Luther, *Luther's Works*, 1:309). For Cain, however, "there was no face of God and no visible sign by which he could comfort himself that God was with him and was favorably inclined toward him—apart from those signs that are common to all beings" (Luther, *Luther's Works*, 1:309).

43. "For wherever Christ builds a temple and gathers a church, Satan invariably has the habit of imitating Him like an ape and inventing idolatrous forms of worship and idolatrous traditions similar to the true doctrine and the true forms of worship" (Luther, *Luther's Works*, 4:236). "For it is the devil's rule to build a chapel next to a church and temple of Christ, that is, to appropriate the works and examples of the fathers, disfigure them, and turn them into a work that is performed without regard to faith" (Luther, *Luther's Works*, 4:237).

44. "Where the Word of God is, there Satan also makes it his business to spread falsehood and false teaching; for it grieves him that through the Word we, like Adam in Paradise, become citizens of heaven" (Luther, *Luther's Works*, 1:82).

45. "For the chief temptation [in the temptation of Adam and Eve] was to listen to another word and to depart from the one which God had previously spoken" (Luther, *Luther's Works*, 1:147).

46. Satan directs his temptation and attack "at God's goodwill and makes it his business to prove from the prohibition of the tree that God's will toward man is not good" (Luther, *Luther's Works*, 1:146).

47. Manufactured religion is "established without the Word by the will of man" (Luther, *Luther's Works*, 2:270); and filling the world with a satanic disobedience; for they prescribe, not what God has commanded, but what they themselves have devised (Luther, *Luther's Works*, 2:273–74).

48. "The papists and Turks are full of faith. But it is an invented faith" based upon self-chosen works "in accord with one's own imagination" (Luther, *Luther's Works*, 4:124).

the works are retained[49] but emptied of their meaning and promise concerning the gospel and the Blessed Seed. Thus the chief attack of Satan, and of all false teaching, is to deny his incarnation,[50] rob human beings of God and his word, and to fabricate a new god.

Therefore, it is God's will that human beings restrain their curiosity and remain within the definite bounds that he has placed before us. They are not to search for something special but are to be content with the revealed word as handed down through the Son of God and the apostles. If we want to have and be his church, his people must not be polluted and commingled with any Satanic doctrine. "The bed is too narrow," observed Luther, for Christ and Satan to remain together. "Consequently, one of the two falls out and the short cloak cannot cover them both."[51]

Larvae Dei and the Harlot Sitting at the Gate

Human beings cannot ascend to God therefore God, in his mercy, ordained to put before us an image of himself[52] so that he can

49. "The world always imitates the customs and rites of the fathers. But it cuts off the head; that is, it does away with faith, the promise, and the command of God and retains the deed itself or the outward performance of the work" (Luther, *Luther's Works*, 4:237).

50. "Therefore he [Satan] does not cease fighting against the ladder and this ascent and descent to draw us away from it. This he sets in motion through all sects and heresies in order that he may divert men from the knowledge of Christ, from His divinity and His humanity, and in order that he may draw the whole church and the members away from Christ" (Luther, *Luther's Works*, 5:223). This is the way that the devil goes to work: one form of attack is to not allow him to be God but just a man; another form of attack is to say that he is true God but did not have the human nature; and a third form is to acknowledge that he is both true God and true man but that what he did was not sufficient to save us. Each of these three endeavors seek to destroy Christ. "Nevertheless, those who are truly godly embrace this light of the Word with grateful hearts and like chicks take refuge under the wings of our hen, Jesus Christ, God's Son, and under them they find rest and protection against every onslaught of Satan and against his stratagems" (Luther, *Luther's Works*, 6:129).

51. Luther, *Luther's Works*, 5:246.

52. "Therefore He puts before us an image of Himself, because He shows Himself to us in such a manner that we can grasp Him. In the New Testament

be grasped. In these signs, he deals with us within the range of our comprehension so that we are able to meet a God whom we can bear. These are the common and public appearances for all Christians; and, in these masks of God, God himself is present.

These signs are also given so that those who do not believe in him might be attracted to him and thereby obtain salvation as they make use of them in faith; therefore, "God establishes a sign of grace in order that it may be recognized by sinners and sinners may be saved."[53] Those who believe the promise and make use of these signs become the people of God.

In contrast to these fatherly appearances of God, the harlot sitting at the gate looks for more attractive externals that appeal to reason and the human eye. Yet "thank God," exclaimed Luther in the Smalcald Articles, "a seven-year-old child knows what the Church is, namely, holy believers and sheep who hear the voice of their Shepherd."[54] "Its holiness does not consist in surplices, tonsures, albs, or other ceremonies which have been invented over and above the holy Scriptures but it consists of the Word of God and true faith."[55] Thus,

> Christ must be sought where He has manifested Himself and wants to be made known, as in the Word, in Baptism, and in the Supper; there He is certainly found, for the Word cannot deceive us. But it generally happens that reason disregards those signs and turns aside to the harlot sitting at the gate.[56]

---

we have Baptism, the Lord's Supper, absolution, and the ministry of the Word" (Luther, *Luther's Works*, 2:46).

53. Luther, *Luther's Works*, 3:107.

54. Tappert, *Book of Concord*, 315:2.

55. Tappert, *Book of Concord*, 315:3

56. Luther, *Luther's Works*, 3:108.

Man Does Not Live by Bread Alone

The person who wants to deal with God must learn that a person does not live by bread alone but by every word that proceeds from the mouth of God. God would have his people learn that "throughout one's life, in every work, and in every situation, one must give attention above all to the Word of God";[57] for the kingdom of Christ is a kingdom of the word, as he calls and rules his people by the word alone.[58]

Satan, the ruler of the other kingdom, strives to draw people away from the word; and the pattern of all temptations of Satan is the same: that he first puts faith to trial and draws away from the word so that a person will listen to another word and depart from the word that God. Thus the fury of Satan is devoted to one thing:

> That he may separate us from the Word, and that we, exhausted and broken either by the multitude or the long duration of the tribulations, may forsake and reject the Word.[59]

The cause of Old Testament Israel's rejection as God's people was her refusal to be led and governed[60] by God. Israel wanted to live, not by faith in the promises[61] of God, but by what was actually present. On the other hand, God wanted her to be faithful and to rely on his promises. Thus they seek what is plainly contrary to the

57. Luther, *Luther's Works*, 3:167.

58. Luther, *Luther's Works*, 8:245.

59. Luther, *Luther's Works*, 5:234.

60. "This was the cause of all the idolatry among the people of Israel. . . . For they wanted to be led and governed in such a way that they did not live from faith in the promise but from what was actually present. On the other hand, God wanted them to rely on faith" (Luther, *Luther's Works*, 8:200). "Thus, God makes promises to His people . . . but at the same time He also tests and exercises them in the faith and teaches that they should live more by the Word than by bread" (Luther, *Luther's Works*, 8:201).

61. "The nature of the promises is that they are given gratis and depend solely on God's mercy, where God alone wants to be the Doer and Worker and demands nothing from us except faith" (Luther, *Luther's Works*, 3:156).

will and government of God, and if at this time they do not get what they seek, they look for another god.

> The Jews tempted Him. When God did not immediately supply them with everything according to their liking and prescription, they quickly ran after strange gods.[62] . . . Therefore they chose other forms of worship and sought such gods as Ashtaroth and Baal, to give them help on the spot and forthwith, without faith in a promise, so that they could feel the help and take hold of it with their hands.[63]

Thus, in order to deal with our sinful tendencies, God offers promises to his people; but at the same time he also tests and exercises them in faith and teaches that they should live more by the word[64] than by bread. For "God wants His promises to be invisible and contradictory, in order that we may be put to the test and exercised, and may learn that waiting is true worship[65] and is most pleasing to God."[66]

> One must be careful to hold fast to the fact that God makes promises and defers the things promised, and that

62. "For so great is the perversity of the human heart that it accepts strange gods far more readily and eagerly than it maintains that this God, who has revealed Himself through His promises and signs, is truthful" (Luther, *Luther's Works*, 4:146).

63. Luther, *Luther's Works*, 8:201.

64. "For if God immediately gave everything He promises, we would not believe but would immerse ourselves in the blessings that are at hand and forget God. Accordingly, He allows the church to be afflicted and to suffer want in order that it may learn that it must live not only by bread but also by the Word; and in order that faith, hope and the expectation of God's help may be increased in the godly. For the Word is our life and salvation" (Luther, *Luther's Works*, 5:202–3).

65. "The true worship of God does not consist in sacrificing cattle, etc. but in holding fast to His promise and believing that it is true and unfailing. This trust is followed by the hope which reminds me that I should wait and that I have a gracious God" (Luther, *Luther's Works*, 4:323). "Therefore, the examples of the fathers teach us what the true forms of worship are, namely, genuine faith, perfect hope, and unwavering love" (Luther, *Luther's Works*, 4:327).

66. Luther, *Luther's Works*, 4:321.

> He tries us with a scarcity of available things in order to instruct us in faith in the promise and in order that this faith may be strengthened and may learn to believe God not only in prosperous times, when things are available, but also in adversity, when things are lacking.[67]

If bread is lacking, a strange god is not to be called upon but, instead, the heart should be strengthened by faith in the word. In all things, God wants his threats to be feared and his promises to be believed and waited for. But this is impossible without faith!

> This is the constant course of the church at all times, namely, that promises are made and that then those who believe the promises are treated in such a way that they are compelled to wait for things that are invisible, to believe what they do not see, and to hope for what does not appear. He who does not do this is not a Christian.[68]

This is the true speculative life of the godly, where reason and imagination fail, where the senses and understanding are mortified with all their powers, and where a person lives solely by the word of God. In our whole life the word is the measure, the standard, and the most precious thing that guides our life. Therefore, "we should arrange our life in such a way that we are sure of walking according to the rule of the word."[69] In matters of faith and life, the Christian must be captive to the word.

67. Luther, *Luther's Works*, 8:201.

68. Luther, *Luther's Works*, 5:202.

69. Luther, *Luther's Works*, 8:82–83. "In one's entire life and in all activities, therefore, one must consider the Word, not only in the church but also in the household and in the government" (Luther, *Luther's Works*, 2:275).

Adam's Why[70] and Abraham's Faith[71]

Simply defined, "it is original sin to become a god. Against this disease we must fight throughout our entire life."[72] It was the sin of Adam and Eve to put themselves in the place of God the Creator and forget that they were creatures. When they were tempted to be as gods, they sought to judge God and, in their asking why, Adam and Eve placed themselves in the place of God when they searched into the reason[73] for God's command and prohibition[74] concerning the tree. No longer were they concerned about carrying out God's commandment as one of his creatures but, instead, they passed judgment upon God himself. Therefore, it became ruinous for them to think about the why and it caused them great harm.

In contrast, Abraham obeyed God's command[75] without hesitation. When God commanded him to be circumcised or when God commanded him to offer up Isaac, Abraham obeyed at once; he did not debate with himself[76] why God had given this command

70. "Therefore let no one add this detestable and fatal little word 'why' to God's commands. But when the command is certain, let us obey at once without any argument, and let us conclude that God is wiser than we are. He who argues about why God gives a particular command actually doubts that God is wise, just and good" (Luther, *Luther's Works*, 3:172–73).

71. For Luther, Christianity involves a very simple relationship: on the one hand, God's promises; on the other hand, a person's faith.

72. Luther, *Luther's Works*, 3:139.

73. "But because he [Adam] turns from the command which the Lord had given and heeds Satan, who discusses the reasons why God has forbidden him to touch this tree, he is hurled headlong into sin and death" (Luther, *Luther's Works*, 3:138–39).

74. "For they inferred that there was some secret reason why God had forbidden them to eat of the fruit of the tree which was in the middle of Paradise, and they wanted to know what this reason was" (Luther, *Luther's Works*, 5:42–43).

75. "But let us keep in mind the example of Abraham. It teaches us that before God we must again become children and not argue how or why God gives us a particular command, but that we must simply hold fast to what God has so commanded and obey" (Luther, *Luther's Works*, 3:171).

76. Abraham, when he was commanded to go and sacrifice Isaac, did not delay; "he did not argue. . . . He listened neither to his flesh nor to the serpent"

but went immediately to the designated place.[77] Abraham considered who it was who was speaking[78] and he simply cut the throat of this baneful why[79] and tore it out of his heart by the roots.[80] He understood that it was God's will that his curiosity be restrained and that it remain within the definite bounds placed upon him by God in his word.

After Abraham had received the command, he saw nothing other than God's command. He mortified the head of the serpent (which is unspiritual reason) and acted on what God had commanded him to do. As evidenced in the faith of Abraham, outward obedience[81] follows upon inward obedience. Abraham heard and believed the word; then he became a righteous doer of works.

(Luther, *Luther's Works*, 4:102).

77. Luther, *Luther's Works*, 3:282.

78. "How, then, did Abraham obtain righteousness? In this way: God speaks and Abraham believes what God is saying" (Luther, *Luther's Works*, 3:21). "Righteousness is nothing else than believing God when He makes a promise" (Luther, *Luther's Works*, 3:20).

79. Abraham "takes reason captive and finds satisfaction in the one fact that He who gives the command is just, good, and wise; therefore He cannot command anything but what is just, good, and wise, no matter if reason does not understand" (Luther, *Luther's Works*, 3:173).

80. Luther, *Luther's Works*, 3:173.

81. Abraham is a perfect example of obedience as he puts his faith into practice with circumcision. "If he had wanted to act in accordance with reason and to argue, he would have said: What is the use of being circumcised in this part of the body? Why did God not choose another part, one that is more honorable?" (Luther, *Luther's Works*, 3:170–71). "True obedience consists in hearing and following the Word of God that is being spoken to you" (Luther, *Luther's Works*, 2:275).

Chapter 4

God's Way of Governing His People

The Life of Noah

Holy Scripture ascribes to man a reason that is not idle but is always imagining something. But it calls this imagining evil, ungodly. But where God is with his Spirit, there is no longer the imagination of the human heart but the imagination of God—there God dwells through the word and the Spirit of God.

During the time of Noah, men were alienated from the word and given over to their lusts and reprobate minds;[1] and the imagination of the human heart was continuously evil. Moreover, the world was filled with violence: there was disregard for all law, with anyone doing whatever he or she pleased and doing it by force.[2]

1. Luther, *Luther's Works*, 2:38. Luther's description of how people lived during the time of Noah was that they sinned "without the least restraint" (Luther, *Luther's Works*, 2:33) and "fear neither God nor men but pursue only their own desires and rely on their own power and strength" (Luther, *Luther's Works*, 2:34).

2. Luther, *Luther's Works*, 2:60.

For 120 years the world was granted time for repentance[3] before the flood[4] would come, as God fixed a definite and adequate time for repentance so that people might come to their senses and escape the punishment. During that entire period Noah exhorted people to repentance,[5] saying that God would no longer put up with their ungodliness; and even though God is long-suffering and patient, nevertheless he will finally punish the ungodly. To his generation, Noah was a confessor[6] who informed others about the promises and threats of God and who was able to withstand the opinions of the world with steadfastness and believe that he was righteous, even though all the rest of the world was unrighteous.[7] Therefore those who keep the word, like Noah and his

3. Luther contrasts two kinds of repentance. There is the gallows repentance, which is to repent "in such a way that I am not ashamed of having offended God but am ashamed because I have done harm to myself" (Luther, *Luther's Works*, 5:152). "For the repentance of the wicked is such that they grieve more about the prohibition of their evil desires and sins than about the mortification of their corrupt desires and sins. These are acts of repentance according to the law, which we usually call the repentance of the gallows. For if he were free of the fear of the cross and punishment, the thief would much prefer to steal than to abstain from another's property. Therefore he grieves that he is restrained by the fear of punishment" (Luther, *Luther's Works*, 6:42–43). True repentance "is to feel seriously God's wrath because of sin, so that the sinner is troubled in his heart and plagued by a desire for salvation and for the mercy of God" (Luther, *Luther's Works*, 5:154).

4. "This was no ordinary rain; it was a rain of the Lord's wrath, by which He intended to destroy every living thing on the earth" (Luther, *Luther's Works*, 2:89).

5. "It is the office of the Holy Spirit to reprove the world (John 16:8), namely, that He might recall the world to repentance and to a recognition of this fault" (Luther, *Luther's Works*, 2:40). "This knowledge of our sin is the beginning of our salvation, that we completely despair of ourselves and give to God alone the glory for our righteousness" (Luther, *Luther's Works*, 2:41).

6. "If you believe firmly and have the Word in your heart, it is impossible for you not to proclaim and confess it with your mouth. Thus the confession of the mouth comes from the word of the heart, so that you praise God, give thanks for His blessings and for the doctrine that has been revealed, and also transmit this doctrine and openly profess it yourself" (Luther, *Luther's Works*, 7:37–38).

7. Luther believed that the flood came about "because the race of the righteous who had believed in God, obeyed His Word, and observed true worship

people, are the church, even though they are very few in number. Consequently, confessed Luther,

> if I were the only one in the entire world to adhere to the Word, I alone would be the church and would properly judge about the rest of the world that it is not the church.[8]

Noah was truly an amazing man, for he alone remained steadfast and retained the true worship of God and lived in the fear of the Lord. He was a man of faith who believed first the universal promise about the seed[9] of the woman; and later on also the special promise about the destruction of the world by the flood and the preservation of his descendants.[10]

The Life of Abraham

It is correct to say that with Abraham a new world and a new church[11] began (even though Shem survived Abraham by thirty-five years), for with Abraham God begins once more to separate his church from all nations, and at the same time he adds a very clear promise concerning Christ, who was to bless[12] all nations.

---

had fallen into idolatry, the disobedience of parents, sensual pleasures, and the practice of oppression" (Luther, *Luther's Works*, 2:12).

8. Luther, *Luther's Works*, 2:102.

9. Noah "had that common faith about the Seed who would crush the head of the serpent, a faith which the other patriarchs also had. Moreover, it was a rare virtue to maintain this confidence in the face of so many corrupting influences and not to depart from God" (Luther, *Luther's Works*, 2:27).

10. Luther, *Luther's Works*, 2:55. "After the verdict has been rendered about the destruction of the world, he [Noah] obeys God, who calls upon him to marry, and believes God, that even if the entire world should perish, he himself will be saved together with his children. This is an outstanding faith, one worthy of our reflection" (Luther, *Luther's Works*, 2:27).

11. "Because the land of Canaan is promised to the descendants of Abraham and Christ was to be born of the descendants of Abraham, it is sure that Christ will be born in the land of Canaan and from the Jews. This light the church did not have before Abraham" (Luther, *Luther's Works*, 2:237).

12. "Because God is good, He uses blessing to mean deliverance from the curse and wrath of God and He promises that this will occur through the seed

Even though Shem was living in Salem, yet the Lord elects as patriarch an idolater who is estranged from God and a prisoner of Satan. For until the day Abram was called by God, he lived in idolatry, had no true knowledge of God, and lacked both faith and the fear of God. "For what is Abraham except a man who hears God when He calls him."[13] "Abraham is merely the material that the Divine Majesty seizes through the Word[14] and forms into a new human being[15] and into a patriarch."[16]

It was through Shem that God warned[17] and commanded Abram to go to a new place; and Abram set out without knowing where he was going. Abraham lived, and was dependent wholly, on the word of God; and according to that word he arranged all his plans and actions. Upon entering the land, Abraham built an altar[18] to the Lord, who had appeared to him. In doing so, Abraham

---

of Abraham, not only for the descendants of Abraham but for all the families of the earth. This blessing the Son of God, Jesus Christ, brought us" (Luther, *Luther's Works*, 2:265). "If the seed of Abraham does this, He must necessarily be a true human being by nature; on the other hand, if He blesses others even all the families of the earth, He must necessarily be something greater than the seed of Abraham, because the seed of Abraham itself stands in need of this blessing on account of its sin" (Luther, *Luther's Works*, 2:261).

13. Luther, *Luther's Works*, 2:246.

14. "The ability to know God comes, not from our innate reason but from the Spirit of God who enlightens our minds through the Word" (Luther, *Luther's Works*, 2:313).

15. "So faith, the work of the Holy Spirit, fashions a different mind and different attitudes, and makes an altogether new human being" (Luther, *Luther's Works*, 2:267). "Faith is a change and renewal of the entire nature, so that the ears, the eyes, and the very heart hear, see, and feel something altogether different from what everyone else perceives" (Luther, *Luther's Works*, 2:266).

16. Luther, *Luther's Works*, 2:247.

17. "Therefore if you desire to be saved, abandon that land, abandon your kindred, abandon the house of your father. Go away as far as possible from those idolaters" (Luther, *Luther's Works*, 2:250).

18. An altar "denotes that a certain place was appointed for teaching and hearing the Word of God" (Luther, *Luther's Works,* 4:89) and "that those who gather there hear the Word of God, pray, give thanks to God, praise God, and carry out those forms of worship which He has commanded" (Luther, *Luther's Works*, 2:284).

appointed a definite place where the church should come together to hear the word of God,[19] offer prayers, praise God, and bring sacrifices to God.

In his ministry as the bishop of their souls, Abraham instructed his descendants concerning the will of God, admonishing them to lead a holy life, strengthening them in their faith, fortifying their hope of a future blessing, and praying with them. In his ministry to the nations around him, God wanted Abraham to bear the sign of circumcision in such a manner that through it the Gentiles would also be invited to faith.[20] For the Gentiles could become the people of God through faith in the Blessed Seed. Therefore, as a distinguishing sign,

> God instituted circumcision which was to be a definite sign and a visible form in the world. In circumcision God would reveal Himself or appear not only for the benefit of the family of Abraham but also for the benefit of all nations. They would see this sign or banner for their salvation, and it would give them the opportunity to come to the knowledge of God. Accordingly, circumcision led to the salvation of many of the Gentiles.[21]

Yet Abraham struggled to consistently live out his life of faith—for example, when he lied and encouraged his wife to lie in their encounter with the Egyptian pharaoh. Abraham willingly and knowingly exposed his wife to the danger of adultery and, by this lie, invited the Egyptians to engage in adultery as well. In so

19. "Thus it is not the stones, the construction, and the gorgeous silver and gold that makes a church beautiful and holy; it is the Word of God and sound preaching. For where the goodness of God is commended to men and hearts are encouraged to put their trust in Him and to call upon God in danger, there is truly a holy church" (Luther, *Luther's Works*, 2:334).

20. Luther, *Luther's Works*, 3:112. "For what benefit, then, was circumcision given? To make known that the Savior was to be born from this circumcised nation and not from the Gentiles. He who was desired by all the nations did not become incarnate among all the nations; He became incarnate among this one people which had been commanded by God to be circumcised" (Luther, *Luther's Works*, 3:91).

21. Luther, *Luther's Works*, 3:114.

doing, Abraham valued his own life more highly than the chastity of his wife and the welfare of others. Yet Luther also believed that Abraham, in putting the best construction on his conduct in that situation, exposed "his domestics, his possessions, and finally also his wife to danger, in order to keep his life, not indeed on his own account but on account of the promise, which depended on his body."[22]

> But the Scriptures reveal that even the greatest heroes of the church were human beings, that is, that they often fell, often sinned, and nevertheless were received back into grace by a merciful God. So these examples are useful both to instill the fear of God into hearts and to sustain faith or trust in His mercy.[23]

Later, when the time came to offer up Isaac at Mt. Moriah, Abraham continued to rely on the promise and that the divine majesty would restore his dead son to life.

> Just as he saw that Isaac was born of a worn-out womb and of a sterile mother, so he also believed that Isaac was to be raised after being buried and reduced to ashes, in order that he might have descendants. . . . For the Word declares that I shall have descendants through this Isaac, even though he has been reduced to ashes.[24]

Abraham had no doubt that Isaac, even if he were to die, would be revived and that his progeny would live on, because God does not permit his command and promise to be of no effect. "God has given a command; therefore we must obey Him, and, since He is almighty,[25] He can keep His promise even when you [Isaac] are dead."[26]

22. Luther, *Luther's Works*, 2:294.

23. Luther, *Luther's Works*, 2:240.

24. Luther, *Luther's Works*, 4:96.

25. "For he who believes that God is the Creator, who makes all things out of nothing, must of necessity conclude that therefore God can raise the dead" (Luther, *Luther's Works*, 4:120).

26. Luther, *Luther's Works*, 4:113.

The Life of Jacob

The life of Jacob is pleasing in God's sight because he has the word, faith, and the Spirit that dwells within him. Hence, God must care for his own who have their eyes fixed on his word. Even though they are tormented and troubled by devils and men, yet God numbers all their actions and thoughts and cares for them in all of their adversities.

Thus, Jacob is a wanderer[27] all of his life, yet he is a patriarch and a saint. In his sojourn he suffers[28] much, especially the defilement of Dinah (Gen 34), with the incest of Reuben (Gen 35), the death of Rachel (Gen 35), and the enslavement of Joseph (Gen 37). Yet God allowed these things to happen so that faith might be exercised and that Jacob would learn to depend on his word and promises alone despite the visible things perceptible to the senses.[29]

One example of how God went about accomplishing his will in the life of Jacob is found in Luther's comments concerning Joseph's servitude within Pharaoh's court after the apparent loss of his son.

> He [Joseph] has not been lost or destroyed; but I am using him as an ambassador to Egypt for the salvation not only of his father, his brothers, and his domestics but also of the whole kingdom and all lands, and in such a way that it is not only a physical but a spiritual salvation, so

27. "For to those who believe and have God's promise, this life is a wandering in which they are sustained by the hope of a future and better life" (Luther, *Luther's Works*, 8:115).

28. "For from early youth and ever since he received the blessing, he was disciplined in various ways. He left his father's house because he feared his angry brother Esau, and he lived in exile for twenty whole years. In exile he endured the harshest servitude under his godless and greedy father-in-law. Furthermore, Bilhah, his wife, and Dinah, his daughter, were ravished and Rachel died. Finally his dearly beloved son was sold and carried off to Egypt" (Luther, *Luther's Works*, 8:92).

29. "For the things which are discerned by the eyes are deceiving and transient, but the things which are promised and not seen are sure and steadfast" (Luther, *Luther's Works*, 6:305).

> that he may instruct the king, the princes and the people
> in faith and in the knowledge of God.[30]

Therefore, in the darkness of the cross,[31] we must cling to the word of God alone. Yet this knowledge of God[32] does not come without practice and experience, so that we might understand that these struggles are indications of his great love[33] and goodness and not of his wrath and anger. These things are done by God so that we might learn what is the good, acceptable, and perfect will of God and be equipped to comfort others[34] in their trials.

The Life of Joseph[35]

Joseph, through his faith, conquered all. First the devil assailed him on the left with all sorts of troubles while he was in exile away from his parents and family. Next he sought to assail him on the right

30. Luther, *Luther's Works*, 8:35.

31. "For he who is not a Crosstian, so to speak, is not a Christian; for he is not like Christ his Teacher" (Luther, *Luther's Works*, 5:274).

32. "This, then, is the true knowledge of God: to know His nature and will, which He reveals in the Word, where He promises that He will be my Lord and God and orders me to take hold of this will in faith" (Luther, *Luther's Works*, 8:17).

33. "The story is told of a peasant who, when he heard this consolation from his pastor, that the afflictions and troubles by which God afflicts us are signs of His love, replied: Ah, how I would like Him to love others and not me!" (Luther, *Luther's Works*, 6:152).

34. Life is filled with trials and tribulations (tentatio); and these drive us to prayer (oratio), asking God for help, counsel, and strength; and these trials and tribulations also drive us to his word (meditatio) for counsel, wisdom, and consolation. It is this kind of spiritual formation and biblical spirituality that comforts and guides us in our baptized life; and it also equips us to be messengers and instruments of the Holy Spirit as he brings us alongside others who are also experiencing their trials and tribulations so that we might pray for, and with them, and bless them with God's word in the midst of their tribulations and struggles.

35. The life of Joseph is recorded so that we might learn the right way to live before God (Luther, *Luther's Works*, 7:354).

with the allurements of the flesh[36] such as lust and pleasure. This is especially the more difficult trial because of Joseph's youth. He felt all of these temptations in the flesh but he was able to overcome these temptations because he had the word of God in his heart.

> From his father Jacob he received the Word which he keeps firmly in his heart—the Word by which he was taught to believe, and trust in, the mercy of God. Through this faith he conquered all. Not indeed that his flesh did not feel those horrible assaults of the trials, since the flesh is very soft and is unable to bear trials or to keep from raging against God. But the Holy Spirit strengthened him . . . and the Lord was with him.[37]

Joseph was well taught[38] by his father,[39] his mother Rachel, and his nurse Deborah. Luther especially speaks of Deborah who was like a grandmother to Joseph and who still had a fresh memory of the patriarchs such as Noah, Shem, and Eber. Isaac too was still alive and he also carefully impressed the word upon Joseph as he recounted the histories of the patriarchs. Joseph also was an eyewitness to the crosses and joys of his father Jacob. It is with this

36. "Now the devil assails him on the right, that is, with the allurements of lust and pleasure. . . . For when youths are about eighteen years old, original sin begins to rage, and there are horrible disturbances and thoughts of promiscuous lusts in their hearts" (Luther, *Luther's Works*, 7:75). Joseph spurned the advances of Potiphar's wife even though it might have been advantageous to Joseph to have accepted her advances, but godly virtues "flowed from the fact that in Joseph's heart the Word of God and reverence for and fear of God were established, because faith reigned there through the Holy Spirit" (Luther, *Luther's Works*, 7:77).

37. Luther, *Luther's Works*, 7:57.

38. "For we see that through the working of the Holy Spirit, that he [Joseph] listened and retained the teaching of his father with the greatest faithfulness and diligence" (Luther, *Luther's Works*, 7:54).

39. "No matter how long God wants to forsake me, I will hold out. My father has taught me to believe and to wait patiently for God's help, no matter how long He postpones or delays. . . . For Joseph had the entire Psalter in his heart, since in actuality and in effect he does everything taught in the Psalms about faith, patience, and waiting. He waits, and he sustains himself with the divine promises which he heard from his father. He does not despair; nor does he murmur against God" (Luther, *Luther's Works*, 7:56).

teaching, and the Lord's presence, that Joseph was kept in the faith while he served in exile. For

> that Wisdom, that is, God's Son, did not leave the righteous man when he was sold but went down with him into the pit and prison. Joseph had Him as a Teacher who gave the increase, so that he kept the Word which he had heard firmly fixed in his heart. He had the punishment of the Flood before his eyes, the burning of the Sodomites, and other disasters, then also the various liberations of godly men recounted by his father. From this source the fear of God, faith, hope, and other virtues grew and were strengthened in him, so that his heart could not be made to totter by any commotions.[40]

Though it seems that all is hopeless for Joseph and that he is alone in his trials and afflictions, yet Christ, the bishop of souls, sees Joseph and cares for him.[41] Therefore, the example of Joseph

> has been set before us in order that we may accustom ourselves to patience, expectation, and perseverance amid evils, even if the delay torments our hearts. For He sees the end of the afflictions . . . Therefore these things have been written in order that we may read, meditate, and learn to bear the hand of God, who visits and scourges us. For the time of affliction is not endless, as it appears to be; but God has fixed definite moments and hours. Only perseverance is needed, as Christ says: he who endures to the end will be saved.[42]

The life of Joseph is an excellent illustration of the manner in which God governs his saints. When he works, he turns his face away at first and seems to be the devil, not God. This is to see his back as Moses records in Exod 33:20–23. "You must see My back, not My face. You must not see My works and counsels with which I am fashioning and refashioning you according to My good

40. Luther, *Luther's Works*, 7:125.
41. Luther, *Luther's Works*, 7:100.
42. Luther, *Luther's Works*, 7:202–3.

pleasure."[43] Joseph beheld his back and waited[44] until God should reveal and show forth his salvation.

Thus the Christian life[45] is one of learning faith and hope in the Lord. In trials we learn patience, faith and hope because our life is hidden with God. If Joseph did not have God's word with him,

> if the Holy Spirit and God's Son had not gone down with him into the pit and had not sustained him with the Word which he had learned from his father, he would not have been able to bear and conquer the assaults of Satan.[46]

Joseph learned that a man does not live by bread alone but by every word that proceeds from the Lord's mouth.

> Therefore it is not due to human help and consolation that Joseph conquers and endures against Satan, the world, and the flesh. Nor does he live in any other life than that which is in the Word of God. For he simply clings to the promise and is prepared to endure even greater evils. Although according to the flesh and also according to the spirit he desires to be freed, nevertheless, because he sees that it is God's will, he rests content with God's good pleasure and mortifies the flesh when it cries out and murmurs.[47]

43. Luther, *Luther's Works*, 7:104.

44. "Why God neglects me in this way, I do not know, but I have no doubts about the excellent, wise and most useful plan of the Father, although the flesh does not see but murmurs and struggles against the Spirit. Nevertheless, the cross must be borne and overcome by faith and patience; for in the saintly fathers I see the wonderful plans of God by which they are ruled" (Luther, *Luther's Works*, 6:352).

45. "The whole life of the godly is one of faith and hope" (Luther, *Luther's Works*, 2:176). "The examples of the fathers teach us what the true forms of worship are, namely, genuine faith, perfect hope, and unwavering love" (Luther, *Luther's Works*, 4:327).

46. Luther, *Luther's Works*, 7:128.

47. Luther, *Luther's Works*, 7:128.

In the cross, he seeks to form you according to his plan. Because Joseph waited on the Lord, he became a savior[48] of the world. God uses all of Egypt to restore Joseph and deliver him from his imprisonment; for Pharaoh and the entire nation are moved by God to serve his purpose and to deliver Joseph from his cross. Thus, the life of Joseph shows to us that faith must precede and then the waiting must follow. Just endure and wait[49] for the Lord; be content with his word and cling to his promises.

This is how God exercises, exalts, and plays[50] with his saints. It is out of his great love for us that he works in our lives in this manner. "For these exercises are useful to this end, that we learn to understand the mercy of God and the mystery of faith and hope and in some manner comprehend the inscrutable plans of God concerning us."[51]

"Like a physician, God proceeds with purging, burning, and cutting, even though this is not done without pain. God accomplishes all this in us for our own good lest we snore through life and perish in our sins. Thus, the cross and trials become the medicines with which God purges away sin. In these trials, it is his desire that we fix our eyes only upon his word and remember that the cross is given so that we might be humbled and learn to wait for his gracious appearing.

The most blessed kind of life is when God does not close his eyes to our faults but immediately seeks to correct us with his rods

48. In the life of Joseph one is able to see "how splendidly God honors and exalts those who wait for the Lord and are able to bear a father's hand and rod" (Luther, *Luther's Works*, 7:174).

49. "For if He immediately gave everything He promises, we would not believe but would immerse ourselves in the blessings that are at hand and forget God. Accordingly, He allows the church to be afflicted and to suffer want in order that it may learn that it must live not only by bread but also by the Word" (Luther, *Luther's Works*, 5:202).

50. "Your life is a game played by God, that all you do and suffer is pleasing to Him, provided it is done in faith, and that finally death itself is precious in the sight of the Lord" (Luther, *Luther's Works*, 7:357).

51. Luther, *Luther's Works*, 6:354.

and crosses.[52] Therefore we must learn to live with our eyes shut and to trust simply in his promises even though he pretends to be sleeping, exercising no care for us.

The Purpose of Trials

This is the doctrine of the entire Holy Scripture, that there are alterations of tribulation and consolation, for God makes his saints sad again after they have been gladdened; thus, one should look for comfort after tribulation;[53] on the other hand, affliction and tribulation follows comfort.[54]

Thus, the word must be learned, and one must exercise oneself in it, in order to know that these continuous alterations are customary in the life of all believers who wish to please God.[55] These exercises of faith are necessary for the godly; for without them their faith would grow weak and lukewarm.[56] For when we are not subjected to trials, observed Luther, Christians forget their

52. Luther, *Luther's Works*, 6:327.

53. "Those who are afflicted by spiritual persecution should be comforted and strengthened with the Word; but those who are afflicted by physical persecution should be assisted with bread and water, that is, with love and hospitality, everyone according to his need" (Luther, *Luther's Works*, 3:184).

54. "One should look for comfort after tribulation, for this alternation is continuous in the life of the saints. Comfort follows tribulations. On the other hand, affliction follows comfort" (Luther, *Luther's Works*, 5:87–88).

55. Luther, *Luther's Works*, 6:99.

56. "The exercises of faith are necessary for the godly; for without them their faith would grow weak and lukewarm, yes would eventually be extinguished. But from this source they assuredly learn what faith is; and when they have been tried, they grow in the knowledge of the Son of God and become so strong and firm that they can rejoice and glory in misfortunes no less than in days of prosperity" (Luther, *Luther's Works*, 5:56).

spiritual exercises;[57] and without a trial we learn nothing[58] and make no progress.

For when there is affliction, we see God "from behind"; that is, we conclude that God has turned away from us and that we have been cast aside by God and receive no consideration or care.

> This is the view from behind, when we feel nothing but affliction and doubts; but later, when the trial has passed, it becomes clear that by the very fact that God has showed Himself to us from behind He has showed us His face, that He did not forsake us but turned away His eyes just a little.[59]

Now you see his back parts, and God seems to be shunning you, but sometime later you will see his front parts and his face. This is what it means for him to love those whom he chastises. This love must be learned from experience, nor should chastisement be avoided and shunned.

Therefore God bestows a blessing "mixed with patience and adorned with reminders of the holy cross; in order that we may be instructed in our trials and learn that our life depends not on bread alone but on every word of God."[60]

57. The main purpose of our afflictions "is the cleansing, which is altogether necessary and useful, lest we snore and become dull because of the laziness and sluggishness of our flesh. For when there is peace and quiet, we do not pray. Nor do we meditate on the Word, but we treat the Scriptures and all things that belong to God coldly or finally slip into fatal smugness" (Luther, *Luther's Works*, 8:7). "For when they are not subjected to trials, they forget their spiritual exercises. Then they pray, believe, and praise rather lazily" (Luther, *Luther's Works*, 8:7).

58. "I didn't learn my theology all at once. I had to ponder over it ever more deeply, and my spiritual trials were of help to me in this, for one does not learn anything without practice" (Luther, *Luther's Works*, 54:50).

59. Luther, *Luther's Works*, 3:71–72.

60. Luther, *Luther's Works*, 5:144.

The Spiritual Exercises of Faith and Prayer

Thus God leads his saints in this life in a manner that one trial immediately follows another,[61] compelling us to exercise our faith[62] and to engage in a life of frequent prayer and praise. Just as trials drive us to prayer and faith, so, when the saints are delivered, they are impelled to give thanks and praise to God for his mercy.[63]

> Just take hold of the Word and bring forth fruits worthy of the Word, and you will see that affliction and trials follow at once. But prayer follows these. Deliverance follows prayer. The sacrifice of praise follows deliverance.[64]

Such was the life of the saintly fathers—it was a life that was full of trials in order that their faith in the promise might be exercised, and that they learn patience in faith and hope. For often in the trial God does not immediately give what we pray for; this happens because he wants to be sought and to be taken by storm, as the parable of the unrighteous judge[65] teaches us.

Therefore we should not immediately cast aside courage and all hope at the first blow, advised Luther, "but press on, pray, seek, and knock."[66] For

61. "For these alternate successions of trials and comforts go on and on, just as night follows day. For in this way the word of promise and faith are put to use" (Luther, *Luther's Works*, 5:55).

62. "Therefore God does this [a person's trial] to exercise our faith. For if He showed us His face from the front, faith would have no place" (Luther, *Luther's Works*, 8:37).

63. "In the first place, one must hear the Word, which is given to us by God. Here we do nothing, but we only take hold of what has been offered. In the second place, one must pray and implore God's help after the Word has been heard and taken hold of, and after getting this help one must give thanks and offer sacrifice" (Luther, *Luther's Works*, 5:357).

64. Luther, *Luther's Works*, 5:6.

65. Luke 18:1–8.

66. Luther, *Luther's Works*, 6:140. "The outstanding example of this is the Canaanite woman . . . who is very well exercised in the speculative life and who presses on in such a manner that she does not allow herself to be repelled by any words, however harsh. She knocks at and pounds the door so long until Christ is compelled to yield and listen to her and to praise her faith and

> God knows the end and outcome of the trial, which you do not know . . . [and] these exercises are useful to this end, that we learn to understand the mercy of God and the mystery of faith and hope and in some manner comprehend the inscrutable plans of God concerning us.[67]

God's Way of Governing His People

Therefore God sends wrestlings, trials, and struggles in order that from day to day we may understand and cling to the promises of God more clearly and certainly. For God rules his people through trials so that the flesh—our own senses, understanding, and wisdom—may be mortified and "that we may accustom ourselves to trust His promises with simplicity and with eyes shut, even though He pretends to be exercising no care for us and appears to be quite different."[68]

Thus God's testing[69] is a fatherly[70] one—"He does not test in order that we may fear and hate Him like a tyrant but to the end that He may exercise and stir up faith and love in us."[71] Satan, however, tempts for evil, in order to draw you away from God and to make you distrust and blaspheme God. Moreover, if the devil

---

perseverance" (Luther, *Luther's Works*, 6:262).

67. Luther, *Luther's Works*, 6:354. "You must see My back, not My face. You must not see My works and counsels with which I am fashioning and refashioning you according to My good pleasure (Luther, *Luther's Works*, 7:104).

68. Luther, *Luther's Works*, 6:359.

69. "God is testing me in this manner, that it may become manifest what is hidden in my heart. It is not that God does not know this, but that I do not know it" (Luther, *Luther's Works*, 4:95).

70. "God knows the secrets of the hearts and the corruption of our nature. Therefore He reproves us in a merciful and fatherly manner, and at length, when the trouble ceases, He reveals Himself to us and says: I am your God, who loves you and lovingly embraces you" (Luther, *Luther's Works*, 8:12). "Then our hearts are gradually buoyed up and find rest in the grace and kindness of God. And this is the consolation of the godly in this life" (Luther, *Luther's Works*, 8:12).

71. Luther, *Luther's Works*, 4:132.

notices that you have the word and are confident that your life is pleasing and acceptable to God on account of the word, he will not rest but will put in your way trials and afflictions of every kind.

Let us conclude for certain, advised Luther, that whenever we are disturbed by various difficulties and by troubles of every kind, consider that God is playing with you. For if he did not embrace you with his fatherly heart, he would not play with you in this way. Therefore let us endure the hand of God,[72] as he laughs and plays with us.[73]

> For God tries us in both respects, with adversity and prosperity,[74] in order that we may be exercised and praise the Lord at all times. Whether He deals with us in a loving and kindly manner or disciplines us, our hearts should be unruffled, and we should give thanks to Him; for He plays with us just as Joseph played with his brothers.[75]

In summary, this is the way that God governs his saints: that they hear the word of God, believe it, and are exercised in faith and prayer by many tribulations.

> God is the Poet, and we are the verses or songs He writes.[76]

72. "Therefore faith in the Word is required, in order that we may be able to endure the hand of God and know what to rely on and where to find rest" (Luther, *Luther's Works*, 8:8).

73. "Therefore let us endure the hand of God, who cleanses us, that is, laughs and plays with us" (Luther, *Luther's Works*, 7:228–29).

74. One of the great trials in life is to become wealthy; for if the Holy Spirit does not dwell in the rich man, he goes along in his affluence and into contempt for God and man, makes flesh his arm, and worships mammon instead of God (Luther, *Luther's Works*, 4:380–81). Thus wealth becomes an idol. Hence it is exceedingly difficult for a rich person to be righteous and godly (Luther, *Luther's Works*, 4:381).

75. Luther, *Luther's Works*, 7:352. "In the same manner Joseph also disciplines and humbles his brothers in order that he may exalt them. Therefore he is the perfect and outstanding example of the governance of God" (Luther, *Luther's Works*, 8:6).

76. Luther, *Luther's Works*, 7:366.

CHAPTER 5

A Series of Theses Concerning the Masks of God and How God Governs His People

THIS CHAPTER EXTRACTS AND formulates selected theses from the text and footnotes shared in chapters 1 through 4 as a means for review, reflection, edification, and conversation.

The Masks of God

Thesis 1

"It is folly to argue much about God outside and before time, because this is an effort to understand the Godhead without a covering, or the uncovered divine essence."[1]

Thesis 2

As a result of our sinful nature human beings cannot see God, in his naked transcendence, and survive. Therefore, there can be no unmediated relationship between God and humankind. God must wear a mask in all of his dealings with human beings.

1. Luther, *Luther's Works*, 1:11.

Thesis 3

This nature of ours has become so misshapen through sin that it cannot recognize God nor comprehend his nature without a covering. Therefore God, in his grace and mercy, envelops himself in his works and seeks to reveal himself to human beings in certain forms.

Thesis 4

"God in His divine wisdom arranges to manifest Himself to human beings by some definite and visible form that can be seen by the eyes and touched with the hands, in short, is within the scope of the five senses. So near to us does the Divine Majesty place Itself."[2]

Thesis 5

In order that God might be known and comprehended, the Spirit of Christ meets us in simple, earthly, and concrete ways. These concrete forms of the Holy Spirit are God's way to us and are a rejection of every way from man to God. These are the common epiphanies or appearances for all people.

Thesis 6

Since the Holy Spirit works nothing without externals, it is the responsibility of every person to apprehend him where, and in what manner, he has chosen to make himself known; for they are the places where he reveals himself and where he is present.

Thesis 7

Since the beginning of the world, divine wisdom has so ordained and arranged things that there is always some public sign toward

2. Luther, *Luther's Works*, 3:109.

which all people might look in order that they might find, worship, and pray to the true God and be saved. Therefore, whoever desires to be saved and to be safe, "let him simply hold to the form, the signs, and the coverings of the Godhead, such as His Word and His works. For in His Word, and in His works, He shows himself to us."[3]

Thesis 8

Outward and visible signs have been placed alongside the word so that human beings, "reminded by the outward sign, would believe with greater assurance that God is kind and merciful."[4] By means of these visible signs of grace, God shows us that he is with us, takes care of us, and is favorably inclined toward us.

Thesis 9

The true God is not a wandering God but has limited himself to a certain place and certain external forms. As God has provided reliable, concrete marks of his presence, so it is the mark of all false spirits to cast aside the external word and signs and to tell God how he must deal with them.

Thesis 10

"Let it be the concern of each of us to abide by the signs by which God has revealed Himself to us, namely, His Son, born of the virgin Mary and lying in His manger among the cattle; the Word; Baptism; the Lord's Supper; and absolution. In these images we see and meet a God whom we can bear, One who comforts us, lifts us up into hope and saves us."[5]

3. Luther, *Luther's Works*, 1:13.
4. Luther, *Luther's Works*, 1:248.
5. Luther, *Luther's Works*, 2:48.

Thesis 11

"This is the first principle and the foundation that is set forth in all Scripture. First of all . . . something, either a word or deed, must precede which moves us, and this impulse must be from God . . . we hear God speaking the Word, and we feel Him working through the oral Word and the sacraments, through which He awakens in us knowledge of Him."[6]

Thesis 12

As God comes to us in these concrete forms, he deals with us in a twofold manner, first outwardly, then inwardly. He draws us outwardly through Christ's word and the gospel and inwardly through the Holy Spirit. Outwardly he deals with us through the oral word of the gospel and through materials signs; inwardly, he deals with us through the Holy Spirit, faith, and other gifts. Thus, the inward experience follows and is effected by the outward.

Thesis 13

"God has determined to give the inward experience to no one except through the outward, external means. For He wants to give no one the Spirit or faith outside of the outward Word and sign instituted by Him. Observe carefully this order for everything depends on it."[7]

Thesis 14

As God works in history, he is disguised and concealed, as a man may hide behind a mask. The history of the nations is the history of an active God who uses the nations as his agents of wrath in order to destroy other, godless nations. Nations do not perish of

6. Luther, *Luther's Works*, 5:258.
7. Luther, *Luther's Works*, 40:146.

themselves, but God wipes them out because of their sins. Hence, history is the stage upon which God executes his judgments and the stage upon which he works his salvation.

Thesis 15

God has ordained temporal and spiritual government as the two means by which he rules the world. Spiritual government is to give its life in the proclamation of the gospel and the salvation of souls; and temporal government is to give its life for the temporal well-being of humankind.

Thesis 16

In the ordered power of the church, home, and government God seeks to govern his world for humankind's good and to reveal, in a daily fashion, his care toward all of humankind. Moreover, it is his desire that he be graciously seen and known as he works all things through his creatures and accomplishes his purposes and will in the world.

Thesis 17

God, in order to accomplish his evangelical ministry of bringing comfort to wounded consciences and leading people into the kingdom of heaven, has always preserved for himself a people who would cling to the word and be the guardian of religion and of sound doctrine in the world.

Thesis 18

God, in his wisdom, foresaw that there would be a great abundance of evil people in the world and that an outward remedy would be required to hold sin in check. Thus, government is God's rod and a minister of his wrath and sword in order to punish all sins forbidden in the second table. Yet, it takes no pleasure in such punishments for it would prefer to have everyone do his duty and not to deserve punishment at all.

Thesis 19

"This, then, is the great glory with which the Divine Majesty honors us: It works through us in such a manner that it says that our words are Its words and that our actions are Its actions."[8]

Thesis 20

"All Christians have been placed into the world for the purpose of serving their neighbors, not only so far as the Second Table is concerned but rather so far as the First Table is concerned, in order that they may learn to fear God and to trust in His mercy."[9]

God's Word and Work: The Ministry of the Word, the Will of His Good Pleasure, and the Will of the Sign

Thesis 21

From the very beginning of human history, through the ministry of the word, God has spoken to human beings through the instrumentality of human beings and angels.

Thesis 22

If you divide all Scripture, as it pertains to the ministry of the word, it contains two topics: threats and promises.

8. Luther, *Luther's Works*, 3:272.
9. Luther, *Luther's Works*, 3:240.

Thesis 23

The law is the word of God that tells us what we have to do and what judgment we have to expect if we fail to do it. Moreover, "it bears witness against us through our conscience, because we have not done the will of God as revealed in the Law."[10] Thus God has given the law in order to reveal sin and to announce the wrath of God and punishment to those who sin.

Thesis 24

This knowledge of our sin is the beginning of our salvation, that we completely despair of ourselves and give to God alone the glory for our righteousness.

Thesis 25

The gospel is the word of God that tells us what God has done for us and for our salvation. This gospel is the good news that we receive forgiveness of sins and become righteous before God by grace, for Christ's sake, through faith in Jesus Christ.

Thesis 26

"Faith alone lays hold of the promise, believes God when He gives the promise, stretches out its hand when God offers something, and accepts what He offers. This is the characteristic function of faith alone."[11]

Thesis 27

Since this faith is a new life, it necessarily produces new impulses and new works. For when faith takes hold of Christ, the mediator,

10. Luther, *Luther's Works*, 2:158.
11. Luther, *Luther's Works*, 3:24.

the heart is at peace; and, "since faith brings the Holy Spirit and produces this new life in our hearts, it must also produce spiritual impulses" through which we begin to love God and to love our neighbor.[12]

Thesis 28

After Adam and Eve had sinned, the Father revealed his heart and pointed to a deliverance through the seed of a woman. It is through the will of his good pleasure that we are able to look into the very heart and will of the Father. "This will of the divine good pleasure was ordained from eternity and was revealed and displayed in Christ."[13]

Thesis 29

"It is impossible for the heart to take courage unless it considers this will of His good pleasure, that is, the Son of God, who portrays for us the heart and will of the Father; namely, that He does not want to be angry with sinners but wants to show them mercy"[14] through his Son.

Thesis 30

In his incarnation, God himself would be present yet hidden and concealed. In Christ, God is found, and outside of the person born of Mary he is not to be found. Therefore, he who encounters this flesh encounters God.

12. Tappert, *Book of Concord*, 124:125.
13. Luther, *Luther's Works*, 2:48.
14. Luther, *Luther's Works*, 2:49.

Thesis 31

If a person is to meet God, he or she must come to Christ. His incarnation is the only view of the divinity permitted and possible in this life. Yet his presence can be seen and apprehended only by faith. It is only by faith, acquired through the word, that a person can cut through the coverings of flesh and blood and see him in Christ's incarnation.

Thesis 32

God is not a naked God but rather one who has clothed himself with definite signs in a specific place. We have need of "signs of this kind, in order that they may lead us to the knowledge of God, since human reason is unable to find God unless such signs instituted by God lead us by the hand, so to speak. And nothing is more dangerous than if one devises his own way to God and relies on his own speculations."[15]

Thesis 33

"When the light of the Word and these signs of grace which have been given by God have been lost, men run, of necessity, after the desire of their hearts,"[16] expressed in their manufactured religions and invented faiths.

Thesis 34

"Now the operation of God is called 'the will of the sign;' for He comes out toward us to deal with us through some sort of covering and external object we can grasp, such as the Word of God and the signs He has instituted."[17] For "God does not rule us in accordance

15. Luther, *Luther's Works*, 3:107.
16. Luther, *Luther's Works*, 1:249.
17. Luther, *Luther's Works*, 2:47.

with His secret will; He wants to do so in accordance with His will as it has been ordered and revealed in His Word."[18]

Thesis 35

As his word is preached, and the sacraments are administered, Christ imparts the word through the medium of human tongues and voices. In the pulpit he speaks through the mouth of the preacher, at the font he himself is the baptizer, at the altar he imparts the remission of sins through the hands of the minister. It is God alone who operates, but he operates through us.

The True and False Church

Thesis 36

God and Satan, since the Garden of Eden, are engaged in a great conflict for the soul of every single individual. God wants every person to be saved and Satan wants every person to perish eternally. As a result of this conflict, two kinds of people are derived from the two sons born to Adam. The whole course of history is the intermingling of two peoples, going back as far as Abel and Cain.

Thesis 37

In the kingdom of the world, Satan reigns and holds captive to his will all those who have not been wrested from him by the Spirit of Christ; nor does the devil allow them to be plucked away by any other power but the Spirit of God, as Christ tells us in the parable of the strong man keeping his palace in peace.

18. Luther, *Luther's Works*, 3:289.

Thesis 38

In the kingdom of God, Christ reigns. His kingdom continually resists and wars against that of Satan, and we are translated into his kingdom, not by our own power, but by the grace of God, which delivers us from this present evil age and from the power of darkness.

Thesis 39

From the very beginning, the Creator ordained that every person be busy with his word and with the forms of worship established by him.

Thesis 40

"The doctrine of the Gospel has been in the world since our first parents fell, and by various signs God confirmed this promise";[19] for "all ages had the knowledge of the Blessed Seed."[20]

Thesis 41

There is a threefold progeny of Abraham: "The first is physical and without the promise concerning Christ. Ishmael, who was born of the flesh of Abraham, was an offspring of this kind. The second progeny is physical, but with the promise concerning Christ. Thus Isaac, too, was born of the flesh of Abraham; but he had the promise. The third progeny is not physical but is of the offspring only of the promise."[21] Sadly the Jews "have lost the true doctrine concerning the promise and faith; and they cling simply to the

19. Luther, *Luther's Works*, 2:163.
20. Luther, *Luther's Works*, 2:163–64.
21. Luther, *Luther's Works*, 4:25–26.

physical birth, which by itself alone is nothing unless the promise and faith are added."[22]

Thesis 42

"Wherever the Word is heard, where Baptism, the Sacrament of the Altar, and absolution are administered, there you must determine and conclude with certainty: this is surely God's house, here heaven has been opened."[23]

Thesis 43

The church is established "that it may be the gate of heaven and that we may pass from this earthly life into the eternal and heavenly life." That is, "the church is the place or the people where God dwells for the purpose of bringing people into the kingdom of heaven, for it is the gate of heaven."[24]

Thesis 44

Wherever the word is heard, there is the church, for it is God's word that establishes the church; for the church exists only where the word is and where there are people who believe the word. Thus, "where the Word is, there the church is, there the Spirit is, there Christ is."[25]

22. Luther, *Luther's Works*, 4:27.
23. Luther, *Luther's Works*, 5:244.
24. Luther, *Luther's Works*, 5:250.
25. Luther, *Luther's Works*, 2:229.

Thesis 45

Wherever the word is, there Satan is active and seeks to spread false teaching by corrupting the word of God in such a way that human beings doubt the goodness of God.

Thesis 46

The chief attack of Satan, and of all false teaching, is to deny his incarnation, rob human beings of God and his word, fabricate a new god that exists nowhere, and to institute forms of worship in which the works are retained but emptied of their meaning and promise concerning the gospel and the Blessed Seed.

Thesis 47

The person who wants to deal with God must learn that a person does not live by bread alone but by every word that proceeds from the mouth of God.

Thesis 48

God would have his people learn that, "throughout one's life, in every work, and in every situation, one must give attention above all to the Word of God."[26]

Thesis 49

The kingdom of Christ is a kingdom of the word, as he calls and rules his people by the word alone.

26. Luther, *Luther's Works*, 3:167.

Thesis 50

Satan, the ruler of the other kingdom, strives to draw people away from the word. The pattern of all temptations of Satan is the same: that he first puts faith to trial and draws away from the word so that a person will listen to another word and depart from the word that God has spoken. Thus, the fury of Satan is devoted to one thing: "That he may separate us from the Word."[27]

Thesis 51

God offers promises to his people; "but, at the same time, He also tests and exercises them in faith and teaches that they should live more by the Word than by bread."[28] If bread is lacking, a strange god is not to be called upon but, instead, the heart should be strengthened by faith in the word. In all things, God wants his threats to be feared and his promises to be believed and waited for. But this is impossible without faith!

Thesis 52

In our whole life the word is the measure, the standard, and the most precious thing that guides our life.

Thesis 53

The task of every Christian believer is to examine what the Scriptures say and see whether what is taught in the church is true according to the word of God. In matters of faith and life, the Christian must be captive to the word.

27. Luther, *Luther's Works*, 5:234.
28. Luther, *Luther's Works*, 8:201.

Thesis 54

"God wants to teach us that we are saved by grace alone and by faith alone. Faith takes hold of the grace that is set before us in the promise."[29]

Thesis 55

"God is interested in faith alone, that is, the reliance on His mercy through Christ. Through it people begin to please God, and after that their works also please Him."[30]

Thesis 56

We teach and confess that a person rather than his work is accepted by God and that a person does not become righteous as a result of a righteous work, but that a work becomes righteous and good as a result of a righteous and good person.

Thesis 57

"God does not have regard for either the size or the quantity or even the value of the work, but simply for the faith of the individual. Similarly, by contrast, God does not despise the smallness, the lack of value, or the lowly nature of the work, but only a person's lack of faith."[31]

Thesis 58

This was the cause of all the idolatry among the people of Israel. For they wanted to be led and governed in such a way that they did not live from faith in the promise but from what was actually

29. Luther, *Luther's Works*, 4:60.
30. Luther, *Luther's Works*, 1:259.
31. Luther, *Luther's Works*, 1:258.

present. On the other hand, God wanted them to rely on faith. Thus, God makes promises to his people but at the same time he also tests and exercises them in the faith and teaches that they should live more by the word than by bread.

Thesis 59

"One must be careful to hold fast to the fact that God makes promises and defers the things promised, and that He tries us with a scarcity of available things in order to instruct us in faith in the promise; and in order that this faith may be strengthened and may learn to believe God not only in prosperous times, when things are available, but also in adversity, when things are lacking."[32]

Thesis 60

"This is the constant course of the church at all times, namely, that promises are made and that then those who believe the promises are treated in such a way that they are compelled to wait for things that are invisible, to believe what they do not see, and to hope for what does not appear. He who does not do this is not a Christian."[33]

Thesis 61

"The examples of the fathers teach us what the true forms of worship are, namely, genuine faith, perfect hope, and unwavering love."[34] Therefore we are to learn that, throughout one's life, in every work, and in every situation one must give attention above all to the Word of God.

32. Luther, *Luther's Works*, 8:201.
33. Luther, *Luther's Works*, 5:202.
34. Luther, *Luther's Works*, 4:327.

God's Way of Governing His People

Thesis 62

"This, then, is the true knowledge of God: to know His nature and will, which He reveals in the Word, where He promises that He will be my Lord and God and orders me to take hold of this will in faith."[35]

Thesis 63

"The things which are discerned by the eyes are deceiving and transient, but the things which are promised and not seen are sure and steadfast."[36]

Thesis 64

"Faith, the work of the Holy Spirit, fashions a different mind and different attitudes, and makes an altogether new human being."[37]

Thesis 65

"If I were the only one in the entire world to adhere to the Word, I alone would be the church and would properly judge about the rest of the world that it is not the church."[38]

Thesis 66

"For the Scriptures reveal that even the greatest heroes of the church were human beings, that is, that they often fell, often sinned, and nevertheless were received back into grace by a merciful God. So

35. Luther, *Luther's Works*, 8:17.
36. Luther, *Luther's Works*, 6:305.
37. Luther, *Luther's Works*, 2:267.
38. Luther, *Luther's Works*, 2:102.

these examples are useful both to instill the fear of God into hearts and to sustain faith or trust in His mercy."[39]

Thesis 67

"In the first place, one must hear the Word, which is given to us by God. Here we do nothing, but we only take hold of what has been offered. In the second place, one must pray and implore God's help after the Word has been heard and taken hold of, and after getting this help one must give thanks."[40]

Thesis 68

The Christian life is one of learning faith and hope in the Lord; for in our trials we learn patience, faith, and hope. "For the time of affliction is not endless, as it appears to be; but God has fixed definite moments and hours,"[41] and "God knows the end and outcome of the trial, which you do not know. Therefore, these exercises are useful to this end, that we learn to understand the mercy of God, and the mystery of faith and hope, and in some manner comprehend the inscrutable plans of God concerning us."[42]

Thesis 69

"God bestows a blessing mixed with patience and adorned with reminders of the holy cross; in order that we may be instructed in our trials and learn that our life depends not on bread alone but on every word of God."[43]

39. Luther, *Luther's Works*, 2:240.
40. Luther, *Luther's Works*, 5:357.
41. Luther, *Luther's Works*, 7:202–3.
42. Luther, *Luther's Works*, 6:354.
43. Luther, *Luther's Works*, 5:144.

Thesis 70

In the darkness of the cross, we must cling to the word of God alone. Yet this knowledge of God does not come without practice and experience; for it is only through practice and experience that we understand that these struggles are indications of his great love and goodness and not of his wrath and anger. These things are done by God so that we might learn what is the good, acceptable, and perfect will of God and be equipped to comfort and counsel others in their trials.

Thesis 71

God leads his people in this life in a manner that one trial immediately follows another, compelling us to exercise faith and to engage in a life of frequent prayer and praise. Therefore the word must always be taught and emphasized in the church, and prayer must always be practiced. For when we are not subjected to trials, Christians forget their spiritual exercises, and without a trial we learn nothing and make no progress.

Thesis 72

God's testing is a fatherly one. "He does not test in order that we may fear and hate Him like a tyrant but to the end that He may exercise and stir up faith and love in us."[44] Satan, however, tempts for evil, in order to draw us away from God and to make us distrust and blaspheme God.

Thesis 73

This is the way that God governs his people: that they hear the word of God, believe it, and are exercised in faith and prayer by many tribulations.

44. Luther, *Luther's Works*, 4:132.

Thesis 74

"I didn't learn my theology all at once. I had to ponder over it ever more deeply, and my spiritual trials were of help to me in this, for one does not learn anything without practice."[45]

Thesis 75

"God is the Poet; and we are the verses or songs He writes."[46]

45. Luther, *Luther's Works*, 54:50.
46. Luther, *Luther's Works*, 7:366.

Chapter 6

How Do I Find a Gracious God?

And Other Questions of the Heart

How Do I Find a Gracious God?

According to medieval teaching, the only secure way of obtaining eternal life lay in the help provided by the church: sacraments, pilgrimages, indulgences, the intercession of the saints, with the way par excellence to heaven being monasticism. At his reception into the Augustinian order when the prior asked him what he sought to find in the monastic way of life, Luther replied, "God's grace and your mercy."[1] Along with thousands of others, Luther became a monk to save his soul and to find a gracious God.

But monasticism did not bring Luther the peace and salvation he sought. While at the monastery, he felt himself the most wretched man on earth due to his troubled conscience. Instead of finding and experiencing a gracious God, Luther believed that he was to do good works until Christ was rendered gracious to him through them. Yet, after all of his labors, who knows whether such things are pleasing to God?

His doubts and fears were heightened by his knowledge of Christ, for the most popular image of Christ in medieval art and literature was the "Christ of the Rainbow." In this depiction of

1. Bainton, *Here I Stand*, 26.

Christ, a "lily extends from His right ear, signifying the redeemed, who are below being ushered by the angels into paradise. From His left ear protrudes a sword, symbolizing the doom of the damned, whom the devils drag by the hair from the tombs and cast into the flames of hell."[2] From this image, along with other teachings about Christ, Luther knew Christ only as a stern judge from whom he wanted to flee, yet was unable to escape. Thus, instead of running to Christ for forgiveness and mercy, Luther would seek out the immediate gods of Mary and the saints. Later on, Luther would realize and confess that all of this was idolatry and false worship.

It was only through the proper knowledge of Christ, based upon Scripture, that Luther found a gracious God. In his incarnation, Luther beheld a gracious and merciful God who possesses a kind, fatherly heart. Luther came to know, through the gospel, that God was no longer angry with him but had shown him grace, and granted him forgiveness of sins, through faith in his Son.

Are You the Only One That Knows Anything? Except for You Is All the Church in Error?

In his debate with Johann Eck at Leipzig, while they were debating the topic of penance, Eck persisted in challenging Luther with this query, "Are you the only one that knows anything? Except for you is all the Church in error?"[3] Yet at Leipzig, Luther could boldly claim with certainty that "a simple layman armed with Scripture is to be believed more than a pope or council without it."[4]

Luther's certainty was based upon the reliable and clear words of Scripture. The Scriptures are certain and clear because they were revealed through the Holy Spirit.[5] However, it was the observation of Luther that the church fathers often obscured the clear word of

2. Bainton, *Here I Stand*, 22.
3. Bainton, *Here I Stand*, 91.
4. Bainton, *Here I Stand*, 90.
5. Luther, *Luther's Works*, 41:58.

God and introduced thoughts and teachings contrary to the word.[6] Thus, Luther preferred "to drink from the source, rather than from the rivulets. . . . I want to have the Scripture in the purity of its powers, undefiled by any man, even if he is a saint, and not spiced with anything earthly."[7]

For Luther, every article of faith must come from Scripture alone and not from the opinions and interpretations of human beings who can and do err.[8] As with Augustine, Luther would believe no teacher unless the teaching was proved by Scripture, even if it claimed heavenly or saintly origin. The task of a Christian is to examine what the Scriptures say, for "no one speaks better than he who understands; but who understands the things of God better than God Himself?"[9] Therefore the Christian is to see whether what is taught in the church is taught according to the word of God.

Fundamental for Luther, the sinner's troubled conscience must have a certain and reliable word of God if he or she is to find peace. Later, at the Diet of Worms, Luther would boldly and confidently declare, "Unless I am convicted by Scripture and plain reason—I do not accept the authority of popes and councils, for they have contradicted each other—my conscience is captive to the Word of God."[10]

Thus, Christians are to clothe themselves with the holy garments, namely, the sacred Scriptures.[11] In matters of faith and life, the Christian must be captive to the word and become drunk by the Holy Spirit.[12] Moreover, every believer has the power to judge doctrine,[13] and every congregation who has the gospel has the right, power, and duty to judge doctrine as his body.

6. Luther, *Luther's Works*, 32:175, 215.
7. Luther, *Luther's Works*, 32:223.
8. Luther, *Luther's Works*, 39:230, 237.
9. Luther, *Luther's Works*, 32:244.
10. Bainton, *Here I Stand*, 144.
11. Luther, *Luther's Works*, 32:139.
12. Luther, *Luther's Works*, 39:307; 41:370.
13. Luther, *Luther's Works*, 39:307, 41:370.

It was with this certainty and resolve that the Lutherans gathered at Augsburg to give their defense of the evangelical faith. As evidenced by their detractors, the possessors of Scripture are the true church, for

> when our confession was examined before the emperor and the whole empire at Augsburg in 1530, some princes of the other side asked their theologians if they could disprove it with Scripture. They answered, "No, one could not disprove it with Scripture, but with the fathers and councils." Thereupon some of the noblemen smilingly said: "Our theologians defend us excellently—they say the other side has Scripture in their favor, but we do not have Scripture in our favor." Out of such an admission and testimony of our opponents we gather that we cannot be heretics because we have, believe, and confess Scripture.[14]

Lyrical Insights[15] into the Fundamental Human Condition: Hungry Heart and Dancing in the Dark

In his song "Hungry Heart," Bruce Springsteen provides ethnographic data concerning the fallen nature of human beings. The

14. Luther, *Luther's Works*, 41:362.

15. Anyone who has attended a rock concert and witnessed the near creedal aspects of the musical lyrics, along with the cultic actions of the performer and audience, can attest that the observation of Francis Schaeffer is true; that is, music is a means through which modern human beings express their views of perceived reality (Schaeffer, *Complete Works*, 5:204). It is, indeed, the hymnody of the world in which the people of the world express their beliefs and design for living.

The value of analyzing the various forms of music, along with their lyrics, is that it permits the learner the opportunity to take note of the language and the thought-forms used and to gain an understanding into the journey of the performer and target audience. This being done, one can begin to understand the context into which the word of God must be sown. Moreover, the contours of the cultural context are expressed in the song's metaphors, thereby providing the Christian with a window of insight and opportunity for dialogue and an evangelical witness of God's word.

It is my contention that God's people, in their study of a world filled with

main character in the song is a man with a wife and children in suburban America. One day he decides to go for a ride, but he never returns home; instead, he experiences an adulterous affair of short duration. In the song he acknowledges that he made a wrong turn in life but, instead of returning home, he just kept on going.[16]

In a different and extremely popular song worldwide titled "Dancing in the Dark," Springsteen describes the modern human condition whereby, as a person looks into the mirror of his or her life, they don't like much of what is being seen; maybe a different look in terms of physical appearance might be the answer. The person turns on the radio hoping to receive some kind of message, but the message keeps getting clearer that he is not going anywhere. In the next stanza of the song, Springsteen observes that the urban jungle, the place where the masses of the world are taking up residence, offers no solution since the street is the place where a person gets carved up and disfigured. In the end, the main character of the song settles for some loving companionship while they dance together in the dark.[17]

As a disciple, I appreciate the metaphors used by Springsteen in the titles of his songs: "hungry heart" and "dancing in the dark." These metaphors find rich expression in the Scriptures and provide ample opportunity for the communication of the biblical message in terms of law and gospel.

For example, David had a hungry heart for Bathsheba. He was so hungry for her that he was willing to kill her husband so that he might have her to himself. Nathan, serving as *God's mask*, exposed the hungry heart of David so that David could possess a

---

false believers, would benefit greatly through a current study of philosophy and music in order to understand the journey of modern men and women, empathize with their plight, and speak a message in the thought-forms and anxieties of the day.

Once these primary understandings of culture have been understood, Christians can seek to communicate the biblical texts winsomely and evangelically to the context through confessional, hermeneutical, and law/gospel understandings and applications.

16. Springsteen, "Hungry Heart."

17. Springsteen, "Dancing in the Dark."

proper and true understanding of his relationship with God. David, in his prayer of repentance and faith, asked God to create in him a clean heart, a heart that would hunger after God's righteousness and design for living. God, in his mercy and loving kindness, filled the hungry heart of David with his grace and forgiveness.

Or, to the people of Naphtali and Zebulun, the region of Palestine where Jesus accomplished much of his ministry, Isaiah said that these people were—to use the metaphor—dancing in the dark. It was to these people that the true light of the world had come.[18]

Why, If Jesus Is Real, Does He Not Seem to Exist Among Us?

The unbelief of a generation is currently being expressed through the lyrics of songwriter Sting in his popular song "All This Time." In the song, Sting relates that only the river that flows into the sea is constant and eternally present. The church steeple in the distant horizon serves only as the dwelling place of birds due to its antiquated and irrelevant message. As he surveys daily life events, he is unable to see God or experience his presence. Hence his question to his parish priest about why Jesus, if he is real, does not seem to exist among us?[19]

Luther's use of *larvae Dei* provides us with a framework for responding to Sting's cynical question of unbelief and despair. As a result of our sinful nature human beings cannot see God, in his naked transcendence, and survive. Therefore God must wear a mask in all of his dealings with human beings. Wherever the visible sign is, there God is truly present wrapped up in the garment of the sign. In the earthly medium of his incarnation, the word, baptism, and the Lord's Supper, God is clothed and meets us through these external means. They are the places where he reveals himself and where he is present.

18. Isaiah 9:1–2; John 1:1–14; John 8:12.
19. Sting, "All This Time."

Yet his presence and activity can be seen and apprehended only by faith. Therein lies the challenge for Sting and his generation. A person may ask, "Where is God?" Luther would reply that God is here among us *all this time* and can be discerned in his masks to those who possess faith; for it is only by faith, acquired through the word, that a person can cut through the coverings of flesh and blood and see God's daily activity and presence in the world.

Thus, in response to Sting and his unveiled seeking of God, those who truly want to see and know him must hold to the form, the signs, and the coverings of the Godhead. In his word and works, he shows himself to the questioning sinner with the hope that the sinner might find life, forgiveness, and salvation in him. It is solely through the Spirit's work and activity that a true and saving knowledge of God can be known and achieved in this life.

When we get to heaven, concludes Luther, we shall see God differently, but here we see him enveloped in an image, namely, in his word and sacraments. These are, and will remain, his masks until the day of his return.

Bibliography

Bainton, Roland. *Here I Stand: A Life of Martin Luther*. Nashville: Abingdon, 1950.

Feuerbach, Ludwig. *The Essence of Christianity*. Translated by George Eliot. Mineola, NY: Dover, 2008.

Kolb, Robert. *Face to Face: Martin Luther's View of Reality*. Minneapolis: Fortress, 2024.

Luther, Martin. *Luther's Works*. American Edition. Edited by Jaroslav Pelikan and Helmut T. Lehman. 55 vols. St. Louis: Concordia; Philadelphia: Fortress, 1955–86.

Pinomaa, Lennart. *Faith Victorious: An Introduction to Luther's Theology*. Translated by Walter J. Kukkonen. Philadelphia: Fortress, 1963.

Schaeffer, Francis. *The Complete Works of Francis A. Schaeffer*. 5 vols. Wheaton: Crossway, 1982.

Springsteen, Bruce. "Dancing in the Dark." *Born in the U.S.A.* Columbia, 1984, compact disc.

———. "Hungry Heart." *The River*. Columbia, 1980, compact disc.

Sting. "All This Time." *The Soul Cages*. A&M, 1991, compact disc.

Tappert, Theodore G. *The Book of Concord*. Philadelphia: Fortress, 1959.

Vajta, Vilmos. *Luther on Worship: An Interpretation*. Translated and condensed by U. S. Leupold. Philadelphia: Muhlenberg, 1958.

Watson, Philip. *Let God Be God: An Interpretation of the Theology of Martin Luther*. Philadelphia: Muhlenberg, 1950.

Wingren, Gustaf. *Luther on Vocation*. Translated by Carl C. Rasmussen. Philadelphia: Muhlenberg, 1957.

www.ingramcontent.com/pod-product-compliance
Lightning Source LLC
LaVergne TN
LVHW020641100826
845148LV00012B/2273

9798385255696